# Contents

I0000269

# Introduction

Your business needs a website. And whether you're selling products, services or your brand, you're selling them online. E-commerce is an inescapable part of entrepreneurship in South Africa right now.

That's why we want to offer you the ultimate guide to e-commerce done right. Heavy Chef and xneelo have come together to offer our best possible advice and tips for the e-commerce journey. We'll lead you from idea to online business, through creating your brand and crafting your content to connecting with your customers, understanding SEO and growing your online brand in the South African e-commerce landscape.

We know the road to entrepreneurial success isn't always a smooth one, but we hope this guide will act as a map so that you know you're heading in the right direction.

Onwards, together!
Heavy Chef and xneelo

# Welcome

You're about to embark on a journey that is fraught with adventure, perilous twists and turns, potholes, ambushes and pots of gold.

E-commerce presents one of the most exciting shifts in business since the first Industrial Age. So many books and articles have been written about this shift that it's difficult to write something new and impactful. In this work, we don't intend to introduce new concepts, but merely to provide a travel guide for entrepreneurs who are looking to take advantage of the e-commerce opportunity. The writing that follows focuses on the art of attracting and retaining online customers.

In the past five years, the breathtaking growth of offerings such as WordPress, WooCommerce and Squarespace has rendered the necessity for old-school hand-coding websites from scratch redundant. Using WordPress, you can get a website up and running quickly. A few YouTube videos later, someone with even rudimentary knowledge of tech can turn their business into an online shopfront. Heck, if you want to be super low-touch about it, you can set up a store page on Amazon or Takealot rather than setting up your own website.

Most of the tricky steps that used to take us weeks to resolve now take minutes – and cost a fraction of the price. Services such as PayFast, Xero and Parcel Ninja integrate effortlessly with all the major platforms. You don't need teams of developers to ensure your website is up. The barrier to entry to setting up a functioning e-commerce website has hit an all-time low.

What does that mean? We're seeing a record number of entrepreneurs entering the online retail space. Every purveyor of products, from apple juice to zapping-rackets, is now jostling, bustling and flaunting their wares on the internet.

The barrier to entry to setting up a successful e-commerce website is at an all-time high. If you build it, they won't come.

This book is not a quick fix. What this book is intended to teach you is the essential threads that weave through your business. Contained in these pages are the bare-bones basics that you need to know – from choosing the right domain name to establishing your brand. We're going to dig into SEO, online advertising, customer acquisition tactics and content marketing.

This guide is also not a silver bullet, by any stretch of the imagination. However, we've put a lot of love and care into providing a concise overview of what we believe to be important to you. It's the top layer. I suggest that you read each chapter, scribble notes, share with your peers and colleagues, discuss the salient points and then apply the lessons quickly within your own business – whether it's a side hustle or your main hustle.

Then, once you've seen the results, iterate.

By obtaining a copy of this guide, you've also purchased a year's access to the Heavy Chef Learning Platform. The top layers of knowledge outlined here can be explored at a deeper level through the thousands of learning bites we're curating on the themes of technology, leadership and creativity. Go ahead and sign up at www.heavychef.com/guides and type in HEAVYCHEFXNEELO in the field that says 'Coupon Code'.

This journey is not about step changes. It's about thousands of tiny little turns of the dial, all combining to propel your business to a position of strength.

Like most journeys, it will be fraught with challenges. If you're resilient, those challenges will be worth it.

Peace.

**CEO, Heavy Chef**
Fred Roed

# From idea to online business

# How to make your business idea digitally compelling

You've got your business plan lined up. You know what your new business idea is going to be, how it's going to improve the world, and why now is the perfect time to launch it. You also know that you need to have a website and an online presence.

But how do you make sure your new business idea is digitally compelling? The internet is a noisy place, and it's sometimes hard to stand out from the crowded marketplace. You can't shout louder than big brands because they have huge budgets for ads. So what can you do? You can be smarter. More authentic. You can hustle.

> So what can you do? You can be smarter. More authentic. You can hustle.

## 5 questions for your online presence

Take an hour or two out of your busy day to go on a thinking date. This could be at a coffee shop, or a walk in nature, or even a long drive. Just make sure you take something to write on because you need to answer these five questions while you have the headspace.

1.  **What's your one-liner?**

    This isn't your elevator pitch, this is literally how to describe your business in one line. It needs to resonate with you because you will be splashing it all over the internet. The more cohesive your online presence is – the same one-liner on your website, social media, emails, videos – the easier it will be for customers to understand what you do, and why to choose you.

## 2.  What makes it unique?

How is this idea or business different from what's already out there? What are
you offering that sets you apart? This could be the people you work with, the angle
you're taking with your service, the product you're delivering or the customer service
you offer.

## 3.  How does it make my life easier?

This is all about your customer. How does your business or product make things easier,
simpler, or more fun for them? What pain point are you addressing? Start with the
customer's problem and how you're solving it. Make it obvious how you'll make their
lives better.

## 4.  Why should I tell my friends about it?

You'll know your idea is digitally compelling when people are talking about it offline.
So what could make people talk about it offline? This will tie into your unique offering
and how you make their lives easier, but it's a little something extra... Think of
Yuppiechef's handwritten notes and what a game-changer that was at the time –
"I ordered this pot and it came with a handwritten note and a little gift!" How could
you come up with something talkable that relates directly to your business?

## 5.  What's your secret ingredient?

This is more than what makes your business unique, it's what makes your heart sing.
Why did you choose this specific business idea, and how are you the right person to
deliver it?

That's your secret ingredient. Think of this as the petrol fuelling the engine of your
business: what keeps you driven, and moving forward.

Once you have the answers to these five questions, you'll have all the ingredients you need
to make your idea digitally compelling. And then it's time for the next step: using these
essential tools to turn the ideas into a viable online business. You've got this!

# How to turn your hobby into a business

So you've got a hobby that you're really, really good at. You love doing it, everyone else seems to love you doing it, and you'd like to see if it's viable as a business.

Maybe your friends have been telling you for years to turn your hobby into a business, or you've noticed that there's a gap in the market for a product or service just like the one you've created. Maybe your work situation has changed and you need to think of creative ways to make money, or you're convinced you're in the wrong job and want to try being an entrepreneur. Whatever your reason for considering turning your side hustle into a business, we're here to guide you through the process.

## Step 1: Think it through

Starting a business isn't a decision to take lightly. While it might seem wonderful to have the freedom of not being tied to an office job, or getting paid for something you love doing, there are practical considerations you need to face head-on.

For starters, are you sure there's a demand for your product or service? Doing some market research (seeing what else similar is available on the market, and what price is attached) is a good first step.

If you charge the going rate for your hobby, will that make you enough money? Is there an option to do it part-time until you get it off the ground, or do you need to give up your current job to do it?

Can you run it entirely online or does it require a physical presence? These are all important questions to ask before you take the plunge.

## Step 2: Decide on your plan

Once you've decided that the time is right to turn your hobby into a business, whether it's because it makes financial sense or there's an opportunity in the market, it's time to decide on your plan.

"It's almost impossible to tackle the big problem from the get-go. You've got to go: what are the small steps that I'm going to take to get to a Minimum Viable Product (MVP)? And then use the data that I get out of that MVP to take the next step."

See this advice come to life by scanning the QR code below.

**CEO and Co-founder of SweepSouth**
Aisha Pandor

## Some things to consider are:

### How people will find you

You'll need a website, social media presence, business cards and a network. What can you do on your own and what will you need to reach out for help with? What opportunities are there to network, both in real life and online? Once you've created your website, be sure to update your LinkedIn, business Facebook and Instagram handle to include your website address.
Set up a newsletter so that interested people can sign up for regular updates (even if this is just your friends and family at first!)

### How your products or services will get to people

Do you need an online shop? WooCommerce is a WordPress plugin that can turn any WordPress website into a shop. Etsy is also a helpful place to test which of your products are popular. If you're offering services rather than products, perhaps you can offer to guest post for other websites that are aligned to your business, to get the word out about what you offer. It's also a good idea to start a blog or video series (either on YouTube or Instagram) to promote your business. Think of where you would look for a similar product or service, and make sure you have a presence there.

Your projected finances for the year

The more organised you can be with your finances, the more of a chance your business has to succeed. How much do you need to sell each month to make your business viable? Keep expenses to the bare minimum for the first year, and consider offering reduced-cost options for first time customers.

Set SMART goals

SMART goals are Specific, Measurable, Attainable, Relevant and Time-based. These will help to keep you motivated without adding too much pressure. Goals are important because they keep you focused on the most important tasks. One of the hardest parts about being an entrepreneur is juggling a few different roles, so the more focused you are, the better.

**S**   **SPECIFIC**     Your goal is direct, detailed and meaningful.

**M**   **MEASURABLE**     Your goal is quantifiable to track progress or success.

**A**   **ATTAINABLE**     Your goal is realistic and you have the tools and/or resources to attain it.

**R**   **RELEVANT**     Your goal aligns with your company mission.

**T**   **TIME-BASED**     Your goal has a deadline.

## Step 3: Commit to working hard

The most important ingredient in any new business is perseverance. It will be a lot of hard work in the beginning, but if you commit to your business and accept that each failure is a learning opportunity, you'll be able to grow and develop your hobby into a successful business.

### Step 4: Keep learning

One of the joys of turning your hobby into a business is the chance to learn more about what you're passionate about. It's also a chance to learn new skills – like how to build a basic website, how to market your business online, and how to network better.

Luckily, you're not doing it alone. There is a community of passionate South Africans ready and willing to help you at every turn – and to share their wisdom.

# Taking your business online (in a hurry)

Now more than ever, your business needs an online presence. While we don't recommend trying to rush things that take time, there are four easy steps you can take if you're in a hurry to get your small business online.

E-commerce is bigger than ever in South Africa right now, worth more than double the R14.1b reached two years ago, according to the Online Retail in South Africa report. Make sure you're not missing out on potential sales by being offline. Ready to start the journey? Let's go!

## 1. Find out where you are today

Before you embark on an online journey, it's wise to take stock of where you are today and where you want to be in a few months and a few years from now. It can help to take a step back to evaluate your brand and what it stands for:

- How do you describe what you do and what business you have?
- Who are your customers today?
- What makes you different from the rest?
- What branding assets have you developed? (These could include your logo, packaging, a jingle, slogan, printed materials or even a colour scheme.)
- How will all of this translate to the digital world? For example, is your company name a good fit for a domain name?
- Are you using any digital touchpoints today? Do you have an online presence?
- What is working well for you and what isn't? Are you measuring all your efforts?

# 2. Planning

Once you have a clear picture of where you are today, you can develop your roadmap for tomorrow. A good place to start is to understand which business goals you aim to achieve by improving your digital channels. Some goals could be:

- Generate leads
- Convert existing prospects
- Build your brand
- Become more visible online
- Proactively interact with existing customers

Think about which customers you want to reach – who is your ideal customer? This can help you to decide what type of website you need to build, the functionality it will require, and how much time and budget to allocate. It can also help to guide your decisions about which digital platforms to focus on to reach current and future customers. You don't have to reinvent the wheel, you just have to be present where your customers are present. Is that Facebook, Instagram, Twitter, LinkedIn or TikTok?

# 3. Build a website

Now that you've assessed where you are today and have a plan of where you want to go tomorrow, you can begin your journey. As you get started with creating or enhancing your digital presence, a professional website can give your business more visibility – in your neighbourhood, across South Africa, and around the world.

To get started, the most important first step is to choose and register your domain name for your website. Your domain name is the part of your website address that comes after the www. Be sure to choose a domain name that represents your business and is easy to remember.

Next, you'll want to choose the tools you'll work with to build your website. A site builder from your hosting company may be a good option if you want to build an attractive yet simple and affordable DIY website yourself. WordPress is a popular option and some hosting companies (like xneelo) offer a Managed WordPress platform that enables you to easily create a beautiful and functional website from scratch. All with demo content and pre-populated themes!

As you get started with creating or enhancing your digital presence, a professional website can give your business more visibility – in your neighbourhood, across South Africa, and around the world.

If you want something more flexible and richer in functionality and features, building a website with WordPress might be for you. You don't need to learn HTML to use WordPress. You can choose from a wide range of free or paid WordPress themes (designs for the overall style of your website), as well as plugins to help customise your site a little more. A range of plugins can also help to boost your site's functionality for e-commerce, for example.

Once you've chosen your website builder tool and the design, it's time to start generating content. You can tell your business's story throughout a handful of pages on your website. Five core pages make for a solid small business website:

1. **Home**

   Make it clear who you are and what you do as soon as someone lands on your home page. This is your one chance to lure in potential customers!

2. **About Us**

   Tell your story – who you are and what makes you unique and trustworthy.

3. **Products/Services**

   A thorough list of the products or services you offer, categorised for ease of reference if necessary.

4. **Testimonials**

   Authentic testimonials from past customers can be a really valuable sales tool, as they show that your business can be trusted.

## 5. Contact Us

The most important page on your website to keep current! Always have an email address, contact number and relevant social media links so that you don't lose any potential customers.

You can adapt these sections and headings according to your industry and as your business grows.

# 4. Expand your digital presence

Building your website is simply the first leg of the journey. Once you have a website up and running, you'll want to attract people to your site. You'll also want to keep talking with your customers and prospects to help generate leads, close sales, retain customer loyalty and build your brand.

> ## "A sense of generosity can go a long way towards building a loved community."

**See this advice come to life by scanning the QR code below.**

authentic
communities
KHAYA DLANGA

**Chief Marketing Officer of rain.co.za**
Khaya Dlanga

There are several ways to expand your digital presence – here are some of the most powerful:

## Social media

Set up social media accounts for your business on the platforms your customers use. Facebook and Twitter are good places to start, but tailor it to your audience. For example, a youth brand may need to be on TikTok and a business-to-business brand on LinkedIn. Post regularly and authentically, and try to respond quickly to queries.

### Blogging

Writing blogs on your own website or guest posts for other sites can be a good way to build your profile and attract traffic. Be sure to promote blog posts on your social media channels, and point back to your website.

### Google My Business

Google My Business (GMB) is a local search platform. It helps you to show up when a nearby user searches for a keyword related to your brand's business, products or services. You can't optimise for local search until you claim your company listing on GMB. If you don't yet have a Google account for your business, set one up so you can configure your GMB profile.

### Email marketing

Promotional emails are one of the most economical ways for any business to connect with its customers. Add a sign-up form to your website to gather email addresses from visitors, and then keep in touch with people who are interested in your latest news and promotions.

While it's possible to take your business online fairly quickly, the maintenance of your digital presence is anything but speedy. It requires constant, steady attention to grow your business online – but it's attention that can reap great rewards.

# Everything you need to know about web hosting

What is web hosting, why do you need it, and how do you find the right partner to enable your business? We'll answer those three questions, right here.

## What is web hosting?

Web hosting makes your website accessible to others on the internet. A web hosting provider 'rents out' allocated space on their servers to their customers for a fee. The cost of web hosting depends on your requirement. The web hosting packages are made up of several features like email accounts, disk space for storing files and the number of visitors allowed (traffic quotas).

# Web hosting package options

There are two main options for web hosting – shared or dedicated hosting. Which one you choose depends on your business's requirements: you may need only a portion of a server or the entire server. Renting a portion of the server is called shared hosting as you share the entire server with a number of other customers. Your hosting provider will continuously monitor all the hosting accounts on the server, making sure that no one is abusing the shared hosting space and slowing the other customers' websites down. If you want every aspect of your web hosting managed for you, including software updates, security patches and networking, then a shared hosting plan is your best choice.

**There are two main options for web hosting – shared or dedicated hosting.**

If you require a lot of disk space or expect a large amount of traffic, you may want to rent an entire server – this is known as dedicated hosting. With dedicated hosting, you have the option of having the server maintained on your behalf (Managed Hosting), or you can manage the whole server, the updates and security yourself (Self-Managed Hosting). In this case, the hosting provider only provides the server and a place in the data centre. You manage all other aspects of the hosting, including which operating system and other software are installed.

# How do you find the right web hosting partner?

Scalability is important when choosing a hosting provider and web hosting package. While you may start off small, you'll want to be able to upgrade your hosting package with ease as your business grows. Be wary of any hosting provider who makes upgrading or downgrading between packages unnecessarily complicated or costly.

You also want a hosting provider that prides themselves on their customer service, and one that makes themselves available to you 24/7. The customer support team should be available by phone and email and should also provide you with helpful resources to guide you if you prefer to figure things out on your own. Ideally, your web hosting provider will feel like a partner in your entrepreneurial success.

# Finding the perfect domain name

"When Hetzner rebranded to xneelo in 2019, one of the biggest tasks we had to accomplish was finding the right name – and the right domain. Our parameters were clear: it had to be available as a .com, no more than three syllables, and it had to be abstract so that we could make it our own. No easy task! We learned a lot during the journey to xneelo, and have compiled all our essential tips to make it easier for our customers to find their ideal domain." says Athena, xneelo brand manager.

## Why the right domain name is so important

Your domain name is often your customer's first interaction with your brand. If the domain doesn't match your brand, or if a brand only has a Facebook page and not a website, it lacks credibility. Your domain name will also be added to all your marketing material – online and offline. Choosing the right domain name is a long-term investment in your brand.

## 5 things to consider when choosing your domain

### 1.  On brand

Make sure your domain name is relevant to your brand, and professional. Before you commit to a company name, make sure that it is available and that another brand isn't using it – or something similar. Ideally, you want something memorable and easy to spell or people won't be able to find you easily. If it's available, register it!

## 2. Creative

It can take ages to find the right brand and domain name. When you're brainstorming, use different sources to get ideas.

- Internal brainstorm: get your team involved in creating ideas – there are no dumb suggestions!
- Customers: ask a select focus group if they want to contribute ideas or which options they like.
- Use an online tool like Wordoid or Panabee that gives you made-up words that sound natural.

It's helpful to set some parameters so that you're as clear as possible what you want the domain name to achieve. Do you want your domain name to represent your company, a brand within your company, an event or a product? Where is your target market? How much are you willing to pay for your domain name?

Once you have a few ideas, shortlist them and ask your team or customer focus group to vote for their favourite. Also, ask strangers what they associate the name with. You don't want a brand name that consistently makes people think of something negative. "Domain names are like surnames: think of Smith vs Smythe. Which is simpler to spell?"

> "Being able to start small and simply and then being able to grow as your business grows is probably the most powerful feature of web hosting."

**See this advice come to life by scanning the QR code below.**

**CEO of xneelo**
Philip Delport

### 3. Simple

Remember that you want your domain name to be easy to type and say. You may need to explain it once to your customers (pronounced "x-nee-lo") but you don't want your customers to consistently get your name mixed up or spell it wrong. A few key points:

- Don't use hyphens and numbers.
- Don't use double letters or deliberate misspelling (switching y/e/l in common words). This may get you a .com domain, but it will also mean you'll be sending customers to similarly spelt websites, and they won't be able to find you.
- Do make it easy to pronounce so that people can visualise it when you say it. This makes it easier to remember and type in a browser, and easier to say over the phone.

### 4. Available domain extension

Now that you have your ideal brand name, the next question is whether it's available... As you'll know if you've tried to buy a .com domain, it can be a challenge to find any available! It's a good plan to brainstorm a few domain extension options.

**Here are some other solid choices.**

- If you operate exclusively in South Africa, use .co.za
- If you're local to one city, consider .capetown, .durban or .joburg
- Choose .africa if you operate throughout Africa
- .co is often seen as the alternate for .com
- If you are an NPO, you can register a .org or .org.za

Don't forget to think of social media as well – it makes sense to choose a domain that is available as a social media handle.

### 5. SEO-friendly

The final thing to consider when choosing your domain name is how it will be seen by search engines. The domain extension signals which region the website is in – so a .co.za website could help rank the site in South Africa. When possible, it's also a good plan to include a keyword in your domain.

# Domain not available? Here's what you can do.

If you're convinced you've got the perfect domain name but it's not available, there are three things you can do.

### 1. Buy the domain name from the current registrant

Buying a domain name is a legitimate marketing expense, and having to buy a domain is a common business practice. As long as you feel it's a fair price for the domain, there's no harm in paying for it.

### 2. Prefix or suffix the domain name

If the domain you want is too expensive, or an international company has the same domain (but a different enough product to avoid confusion), you can always add a verb or noun to the beginning or end of the domain.

- Verb: godomainname.com or buydomainname.com
- Noun: domainnameapp.com domainnamemag.com
- Region: domainnamesa.com domainnamecapetown.com

### 3. Choose an aligned domain name

If your brand name is taken, you can always use your company slogan or motto, or a unique sub-brand name. Try to think laterally, and be as creative as possible.

> "I think the best ideas are not always the best ideas in the moment. Sometimes you've got to play with multiple things and one of them will gain traction."

**See this advice come to life by scanning the QR code below.**

**Co-founder of Yuppiechef.com**
Andrew Smith

So there you have it: a few helpful tips for finding the right domain for your business. Once you have it, you'll need to register the domain name and set up your web hosting. And then it's time to share your brand with the world!

# Must-have tools to grow your business online

Whether you've just started a business, moved your business online, or need to give your online presence a boost, we know that it can seem a little overwhelming. Running a business is no easy feat – it takes courage, perseverance and resources.

## Define your brand story

Conventional branding includes your logo, business cards and your storefront or office branding. Now that you're taking your business online, the most important element of your brand is your website. Visitors need to know, as soon as they land on your website, what you're offering them and why they should choose you.

Customers are inundated with product and service offerings – you need to cut through all the online 'noise'. How do you do that? By standing out from the crowd. Think of some of your favourite brands – what sets them apart? The answer probably lies in their brand story – a short one-liner that tells their customers what makes them special. What's your brand story?

Customers are inundated with product and service offerings – you need to cut through all the online 'noise'.

One element of your brand story will focus on your products and services – why you chose to start this particular business. Your founding story. The other element should focus on what sets you apart – what are your unique selling points and how do they differ from your competitors? Remember, your website is your online business card so it needs to look professional.

# Promote your website

Oftentimes, the more money you put into your marketing, the greater return on investment you'll see. But sometimes, when you're a small business, your marketing budget may be quite limited. Luckily, there are plenty of ways you can promote your business online without breaking the bank. Here are some of them:

### 1. Reach out to bloggers or influencers

Ensure they share the same audience and interests as you. Send these influencers free samples of your products or offer them a free trial of your service to review. Customers tend to trust real reviews over sponsored posts.

### 2. Create quality content

Then share it on your blog. Blogging is probably the best low-cost method of promotion as it's easy to scale as your business does. It's also fairly easy to start a blog (if you use a platform like WordPress). Start by publishing one blog post a week and then ramp it up as you're able. But remember, with content, consistency is key.

### 3. Improve your SEO

High-quality content with SEO (Search Engine Optimisation) helps search engines (like Google) find your website. This means that other people searching the web are more likely to find your website as well. One way to improve your SEO is by publishing high-quality content.

# Use Google's tools

## Google My Business

One of the most valuable tools you can have in your business toolbox is Google My Business – a free business listing tool. When customers search for your business on Google Search or Google Maps, it will appear in the search results along with your location, contact details and any other relevant information.

This is the ideal platform to promote your services, physical address, opening hours, photos and customer reviews – free of charge. Once set up, don't forget to ask your customers to review your products and services. This isn't the only valuable tool Google provides for small businesses, you can find out more on their Google for Small Business platform.

## Google Ads

When used correctly, Google Ads provide huge reach and potential sales for your business. The two most popular choices of advertising on Google Ads are search ads (ads that show in response to search queries on Google) and display ads (banner ads displayed on websites).

What makes Google Ads even more attractive is the fact that you're able to monitor and measure where every rand goes. That way, if a campaign isn't working, you can adjust your spend or even pause the campaign while you make improvements to your selling proposition. No long term commitments! It's a good idea to try a few different campaigns to see what works best for your business. When you find that 'sweet spot', you can increase your spend on it.

## Google Analytics

Google Analytics is a free tool but there is also a paid-for version that includes more in-depth functionality. Google Analytics helps you track visitors to your site and understand their behaviour – which pages they landed on, the time they spent on those pages and any other actions they took while browsing your site.

Once you understand how your visitors interact with your website, you can optimise it to perform better. By tracking where your visitors dropped off, you'll know where to fix any issues they may be experiencing in the user journey. You can find out where your visitors came from and tailor your products and services to match them more effectively. You can also check Google Search Console, which provides insight into how your website is performing.

## Ensure you're visible online

If your customers can't find you, they can't buy from you or use your services. One of the many important tasks you face as a small business owner is making sure your website is immediately visible so that customers can easily find you. One important way to do this is to use content marketing to rank higher and attract visitors.

Content marketing is the process of creating authoritative, relevant, and unique content to attract visitors. The goal of content marketing is to provide content that your customers need, and want to engage with. You can distribute this content via multiple channels (your website, newsletter, social media channels and ads). Thoughtful, informative content that provides value to your target market has a strong chance of ranking well with search engines and drawing customers to your site.

## Make your mark on social media

Now that you're online, you need to be on social media (if you aren't already!). First prize is having your social media handles match your domain name exactly (website address), but this isn't always possible. Remember to keep your social media handles professional and memorable – you want it to be easy for your customers to remember when they need to.

There's never been a better time to grow your business online. With the right tools, this process doesn't need to be as daunting as it was in the past. Starting a business is the hardest part – we're here to help you as you grow.

# Napkin notes:
# From idea to online business

**Your idea needs to be digitally compelling so that your brand can stand out from the noise online. To create this, you'll need to do some deep thinking and creating.**

Planning is essential. Once you know where your business is, you can figure out where you need to go, and how you need to grow online.

A professional website is an essential first step. This should be supported by a reliable web hosting partner.

Choosing the right domain name is an important branding exercise – take your time with it.

Authenticity is essential at every stage of the e-commerce journey.

---

---

---

---

---

---

---

---

---

---

---

---

---

# 02

# Creating your brand

# Building an online brand

Once you have your website and social media set up, what's next? It's time to start building your online brand.

Your brand encapsulates everything about your product or service. It's the thing itself, of course (the product or service), but it's also the way you make people feel and the way you communicate with them, how you connect with them and what you add to their lives. If you want to build a powerful brand online, there are three things to remember.

## The 3 Cs for online branding

The 3 Cs are a simple way to check that you're looking at the big picture when it comes to online branding. They are Creativity, Caring and Consistency. Let's dive into each in a little more detail.

### 1.  Creativity

There is something that you – and only you – have to say. Some specific niche that your brand fills. What is it? Why did you start your company and what is your USP (Unique Selling Point)? Once you know this, you'll know what you're uniquely qualified to share. Then you can build your content around this – whether it's a blog or website article, social media updates, video or a podcast. A big part of this is finding your brand story.

Think big: what problem can you solve for your customers, what do they need to hear from you (and only you) and what is the best way to communicate this message? Then think small: how can you start this online branding journey today? Make it specific, and measurable. (We all love SMART goals: Specific, Measurable, Attainable, Relevant and Time-based.)

Creativity is necessary to find the exact niche that you can fill online. You want it to be one that fills you with excitement and purpose. One that feels like you have something relevant and helpful to add to the internet. Once you've tapped into that, you can let it shine through your brand.

Creativity is necessary to find the exact niche that you can fill online. You want it to be one that fills you with excitement and purpose.

## 2. Caring

This brings us to our next point: caring. We are all maxed out on information and products and services. The internet has brought us many blessings, but it has also brought us a lot of noise – much of which feels unnecessary. How can you be caring towards your customers? How can you be mindful of their cognitive load and only give them relevant, helpful information?

Seeing customers as people (rather than just walking wallets) is helpful because it makes you consider their daily desires and frustrations. Think of ways that your brand can plug some of those frustrations, and make their lives easier.

How can you be caring towards your customers? How can you be mindful of their cognitive load and only give them relevant, helpful information?

## 3. Consistency

And finally, be consistent. It might sound boring, but consistency is what builds a solid foundation for an online brand. If you post a brilliant article one week and then nothing for a few weeks, and then a fairly random article, you're not going to build a following.

Consistency is important not just in routine, but also in personality. Think about the foundational attributes of your brand, and stick to them. Let your customers know what to expect from your brand's personality – what kind of content you post, what niche you fill, and what problems you can help them to solve.

If you have a posting schedule that you stick to, and offer nuggets of wisdom or practical tips or helpful insights to your potential customers every week (or day!) at the same time, they will come to expect that from you. They'll come to depend on it.

> "Consistency comes when your message, knowledge and way of living are consistent. I want to get to a place where I'm able to look at myself in the mirror and be satisfied with the most authentic version of myself."

**See this advice come to life by scanning the QR code below.**

**Media Personality at**

**mapsmaponyane.com**

Maps Maponyane

# Online branding sense check

So there you have it: your sense check for online branding.

- The first step, of course, is setting up a professional website. Your website should be hosted by a reliable web hosting company that can help you achieve your business goals.
- The next step is to write meaningful content that will appeal to your customers and to ensure your SEO strategy is solid.
- And finally, keep in mind, at all times, that your customers are every bit as busy and human as you are, so what you offer should make their lives easier, and sweeter.

# How does your brand speak? A step-by-step style guide.

When you're building your brand, consistency is essential. Both in your service delivery and your communication style. A brand style guide can help you maintain consistency, every day – here's how to create one, step-by-step.

## What is a brand style guide?

A brand style guide is a reference for all elements of your brand: visuals, aesthetics and voice. Let's take a look at how your brand speaks, and how to create a style guide for communication.

But before we get into the ins and outs of creating a style guide, do you know why you need one in the first place? When you're building your brand, consistency is everything. A consistent voice helps potential customers develop brand recognition, which means they're more likely to remember your unique selling points when it comes to making buying decisions. The best way to ensure consistency across every platform is by creating a brand style guide.

**A style guide is a set of guidelines that clearly defines your brand's communication style.**

## Communication rulebook

A style guide is a rulebook that clearly explains the way your brand communicates – internally and externally – to ensure uniformity throughout all the different communication channels you use.

# This guide should include:

- Your tone (the way you speak to customers). For example, are you a friendly adviser or an informed expert?
- Any specific product terminology or brand phrases. Do you use acronyms or spell out the word?
- The way you address customers in your communication. Do you address them by their first name?
- A complete grammar list so that things are spelt consistently throughout all your communications.

# Work in progress

Your style guide will always be a work in progress and it will need to be updated from time to time. As language evolves, so will your company, and your style guide will need to be kept as up to date as possible – which means regular revisions and reviews.

**When it comes to your brand's voice, your style guide is your source of truth.**

# Tell your story

Before you can decide on your brand voice, you need to understand your brand story. Your brand story is a summary of all the things that make your business unique: your vision, mission and values.

When you start to work through these fundamentals, certain traits will reveal themselves: what makes your brand stand out from the rest. These traits will help you define your brand's personality.

Your brand personality and voice must be one that your customers can relate to. For example, the brand personality of a medical supplies company would be very different from a company that sells travel packages. This personality will determine your communication style and tone.

> Your brand story is a summary of all the things that make your business unique: your vision, mission and values.

**To find your brand story, ask yourself these questions:**
- What are our values?
- What is our company vision and mission?
- How are we different from other businesses in the same industry?
- How do we want our customers to feel about our brand?
- How do we make our customers' lives better?
- How should we communicate with our customers? How do they communicate?

# Build your voice

Building your online voice won't happen overnight – it's a slow process and consistency is key. Be authentic in your communication, especially on social media. Engage with your customers, don't speak at them. Customers are bombarded with communication in the digital landscape. Be gentle with them.

Focus on the way you communicate with your audience: make your communication more human by being as relatable as you can. This will help your audience to be more receptive to the message you're communicating.

> When you're crafting your brand voice, be timeless, not trendy.

# Brand voice essentials

- Your online voice should be genuine.
- All communication from your company should be consistent.
- Brand voice guidelines should be established and shared with everyone in your company.

Now that you know what a style guide is – and why it's essential to have one – here are 4 steps to create yours.

# 4 steps to craft your style guide

## 1. Know your audience

If you want your audience to listen to you, you need to relate to them. To do this, take the time to understand who your audience is.

- How old are they?
- Where do they live?
- Are they mostly male or female?
- What does a typical customer look like?
- Are your potential customers local or international?

"When crafting any business message, the first step is a simple one. It's: 'what is the purpose of this thing?'

Do you want to inspire, educate, enlighten, entertain, persuade? If your purpose isn't clear, it may be too soon to start writing. Sure, you can have more than one purpose, or combined purposes, but there should be one dominant purpose."

**See this advice come to life by scanning the QR code below.**

**Founder of**
**tiffanymarkman.co.za**
Tiffany Markman

## 2. Clearly define your tone

Your tone is not only what you say, but how you say it. Make sure that the words you use don't inadvertently exclude anyone from your content. Be as inclusive as possible without losing your audience.

Avoid using industry jargon that customers may not understand – communicate simply. Your audience doesn't want to struggle to understand your message. Keep them engaged by being brief and to the point.

## 3. Decide on your communication style

Just like we all have our own way of talking when we're chatting in person, your brand needs to have one too. This includes everything from the way you create your content to the way it's laid out on your website. It's essential that these decisions are made upfront, and clearly documented so your content team can be consistent.

Consider the following:
- Is your communication style formal or more casual?
- Do you write long-form content or short and snappy?
- How do you lay out your content? When do you use bold or italics? When do you use numbering or bullet points?
- Do you use visuals in your content? Illustrations, photos or infographics?

### 4. Establish a content structure

When you know what you want to communicate and to whom, the last piece of the puzzle is establishing guidelines for the way you structure this content. Outline any rules you have around titles and subtitles, heading structure and article structure.

Does this seem a bit overwhelming? The best advice is to start as soon as possible, keep it simple, and be prepared to make revisions often. As you grow, so will your voice. Update your content style guide whenever necessary, and make sure that everyone is aware of these updates. Consistency in communication builds trust over time.

Build your style guide one decision at a time and you'll lay a solid foundation for speaking to your customers.

# Golden rules of content marketing

The phrase 'content marketing' is thrown around a lot these days. But do you know what it is, and how you should be using it for your small business? There are a few golden rules of content marketing that can make a big difference to your business – we've outlined them for you here.

## What is content marketing?

Essentially, content marketing means using your content as a marketing tool. Providing relevant, helpful information to your potential customers – in whatever format you choose – that positions you as an expert. It's important to be authentic in your content marketing. You're not advertising false claims or promising quick wins: you are authentically sharing your knowledge and expertise to make your customers' lives easier.

# The golden rules: connect, create, share

There are three golden rules to content marketing, to ensure that you're getting the most out of your efforts. While you could see content marketing as just another SEO tactic – and there's no doubt that it's very helpful for your SEO – at its core, it's more about connecting to your customers in ways that are authentic and meaningful. Let's take a closer look at each of these rules.

There are three golden rules to content marketing, to ensure that you're getting the most out of your efforts.

## Connect

The first decision you have to make when deciding on a content marketing strategy is where you want to focus your efforts. It takes a lot of time to create meaningful, helpful content that is high quality and relevant – and that's the only kind of content you want on your site. There is no point churning out fluff that's peppered with the right keywords or getting low-cost bulk content to fill up your site. We are all too busy and the internet is already too crowded. You owe it to yourself and your customers to focus your attention where it can be really helpful.

So where are your customers, mostly? Do they come to your website, and if so would they prefer blog-style articles or videos? Do you interact mostly on Facebook? If so, would they prefer content in infographics or lists, or are they likely to click through to a longer-form article? If most of your customers are following you on Instagram, you'll want to tailor your content to be beautiful and keep the links to a minimum, because Instagram is not link-friendly. Engagement via comments can be very high if you're asking the right questions, though. If you're connecting with potential customers on LinkedIn, you can choose to link to the content on your site or to write LinkedIn articles.

There are all kinds of options here. Yes, it's a good plan to have them live on your website or social media platforms. Yes, it's a good idea to include them in your newsletter so that your existing customers can upskill themselves. But how else can you disperse your content? How can you broaden your content marketing net?

> You owe it to yourself and your customers to focus your attention where it can be really helpful.

Deciding where to connect to your customers and in what format (writing, video, images, infographics) is an essential first step. Don't be afraid to ask your customers, too – if you have a newsletter or an active social media account, ask for feedback. This is also a great way to crowd-source ideas for content: you can ask what information people are looking for, or if they have any questions for you. The responses you get can feed into your content marketing plan.

## Create

Think about what you're an expert in. What specific information or knowledge would you like to share with your customers? How could you make their lives easier? Once you've zeroed in on your topics, you can create content around what would help your customers to do their job quicker or more effectively.

This will look completely different for every company, and that makes sense. Perhaps you sell a technical product or service, and you can speak in advanced jargon because you know your customers speak the same language. Maybe you're launching a mass-market product and you need to appeal to the similarities in all of us – that will be a very different kind of content. Tap into what makes your customers unique, and what you have to offer them, and focus on that. Think of each piece of content you create as adding to your brand story, writing another chapter in your brand book.

> Tap into what makes your customers unique, and what you have to offer them, and focus on that.

If you've been running your business for a while, you can also think back to the things you wish you'd known in the beginning, and share insights about those aspects of your business. Think of it as a mentoring path, a way to show that your success was built step-by-step. What seems obvious to you now may be revolutionary for someone who has recently started. And, of course, don't be shy to share the stories of your customers and clients if they have given testimonials.

> One caution when it comes to sharing specific knowledge: try to ensure that you're being as inclusive as possible. Not all of your customers will have the same background as you, so if there's anything that might not be obvious, try to link to an FAQ or Glossary section. Similarly, if you're working mainly with visuals, be sure to include both genders, all races and different ages so that you're not excluding an important part of your customer base.

## Share

So now you've crafted your beautiful video, or you've written your series of articles or designed your infographics that explain everything you need to know about your specific niche. Now what? This is the fun part – you get to figure out how to share them with your customers and your future customers.

> Content marketing might be as simple as starting a blog, or as ambitious as starting a podcast.

You might choose to turn some of your articles into an e-book and offer it as a free download when people sign up for your newsletter. You could share it on your social media, or offer a shorter version of an online course as a free masterclass. Perhaps you could design an infographic that shares all the must-know secrets about a certain topic and post it to groups interested in that topic on Facebook. The options are endless, once you have the collateral to work with.

Content marketing might be as simple as starting a blog, or as ambitious as starting a podcast. It might be part of your daily work or something that you enlist outside help with. What is important is that you have a clear plan for what content you want to share and that you know exactly where – and how – to share it.

With the right plan, content marketing can be just one more way to empower your small business to great success. That's what we're rooting for.

# Napkin notes:
# Creating your brand

1. Remember the 3 Cs for online branding: Creativity, Caring and Consistency.
2. When it comes to your brand's voice, your style guide is your source of truth.
   A style guide is a rulebook that explains the way your brand communicates.
3. You need to have a clear content strategy to ensure you're spending your time wisely
   and communicating effectively with your customers.
4. The golden rules of content marketing are: connect, create, share.
5. Meet your customers where they are: on the platforms you're already interacting
   with them on.

# 03

# Crafting content

# A step-by-step guide to content strategy

If you understand the golden rules of content marketing, and you're working hard to connect with your customers, you may feel as if that's enough focus on content for now. But do you have an overarching content strategy? Here's a step-by-step guide so you can answer that question.

## 1. Decide which gap you are filling

The first step in creating your content strategy is deciding which questions you are answering. The visitors to your site have a specific set of questions or are trying to solve a particular problem. What is this gap, and why are you uniquely placed to fill it?

> "Above all else, be brave, be courageous, be different, be something else."

**See this advice come to life by scanning the QR code below.**

word-of-mouth marketing
MONGEZI MTATI

**Founder and Managing Director of wordstart.co.za**
Mongezi Mtati

## 2. Know who your customers are

It's important to have a deep understanding of who your customers are so that you can offer them the content they need. It can be helpful to create a persona of a typical customer: outlining their age, gender, where they live, what kind of work they do, how they access the internet and why they need the product or service that you offer.

You may have a few different types of customers, in which case you'll create a few different personas. Give them made-up names, and then you can reference them when you're making content decisions. "Would Sarah understand this lingo? Does Siya need more detail here?"

It's important to have a deep understanding of who your customers are so that you can offer them the content they need.

## 3. Choose what type of content you will produce

Now that you know what you want to share, and who you want to share it with, it's time to decide what format the content will be in.

- Are you going to be writing articles (long or short)?
- Are you going to create videos?
- Are you going to drive your content through social media, and if so, which platforms?
- Are you going to focus on stories (for Facebook, Instagram and Google)?
- Do you think a newsletter would work best?

There are so many different kinds of content available online today, and knowing which ones your customers will respond to will influence your content strategy. If you're not sure, you can always test out a few different options and see which one has the most engagement.

## Plan out your content

Once you've decided on the format, it's time to think about the frequency, and plan a content calendar. Consistency is essential: your customers will come to recognise that you are offering advice or guidance on a certain topic at a certain time, and the goal is to become their go-to for this specific kind of information. If you post sporadically, this is less likely to happen.

It can help to choose specific themes for each month (within your broader content themes) and then break those themes down into questions that you answer each week. Ideally, you want to know ahead of time exactly what your content calendar looks like for the next three months.

> The goal is to become your customers' go-to for a specific kind of information.

## Distribute it through your channels

Now that you have a consistent posting schedule, be sure you're distributing it as far and as widely as possible. Remember the three rules of content marketing: connect, create, share. There's no point creating the ideal content if you're not able to share it effectively. You could share through your website, social media, newsletter, WhatsApp or any other ways you have to connect to your customers.

A content strategy takes your brand story, combines it with content marketing, and produces something truly helpful for your customers. Think of it as a guide that ensures you're answering all the necessary questions in a way that builds your brand.

# A guide to creating and managing your content calendar

A content marketing strategy is essential for small business owners today – but you can't just share any piece of content on any platform without thought. Having a content calendar means you're strategic with what to share, when.

Creating a content calendar from scratch may seem overwhelming – especially if you haven't done it before. But once you understand the process, it's fairly easy to replicate.

# Using content to find customers

When you build a website, the main aim is for your customers – and potential customers – to find you easily. Sadly, this won't just happen automatically – you need to optimise your content for search engines, like Google, to find you. One way of doing this is through Search Engine Optimisation (SEO). A fairly easy win in terms of SEO is publishing regular, fresh, high-quality content on your website or blog. You can also share these content pieces on social media to expand your reach and generate more traffic to your site.

In fact, blogging is one of the most effective ways to help grow your business. According to HubSpot, 82% of marketers who blog see a positive return on investment (ROI) from inbound marketing.

# Benefits of a content calendar

Consistency is essential when building an audience: you want your readers to know what to expect from you, and when. A content calendar is a predetermined content plan that explains which content pieces you'll post when, and why. In short, it's an editorial schedule that helps you prepare in advance the type of content you'll distribute.

**82% of marketers who blog see a positive return on investment (ROI) from inbound marketing.**

You can decide how far in advance you'd like to plan your content according to your content strategy, but we'd recommend at least three months in advance.

**Using a content calendar can help you to:**
- Keep your posting schedule organised and consistent.
- Reduce the risk of forgetting to post new content as planned.
- Make it easier to plan content around important dates, like holidays or relevant events.
- Provide a visual workflow for creating content on a daily, weekly or monthly basis.

# Creating a content calendar

The most challenging aspect of creating your content calendar is lining it up with your content marketing key objectives. It's a good idea to set aside some time to brainstorm a few ideas and then decide on the most relevant, helpful and interesting pieces.

If you're at a loss for ideas, don't worry. To help you feel inspired, consider:

- Researching competitors or industry giants to see which topics their readers respond well to.
- Analysing your analytics to determine which articles have performed the best or had the most engagement on your platforms.
- Using a tool (like Buzzsumo) to source popular content related to your audience interests.
- Browsing frequently asked questions (FAQs) customers have submitted to you in the past and creating content around these answers.

Once you've decided on the topics, start scheduling them into your content calendar so you can plan accordingly. There are even scheduling tools you can use if you don't have time to do it manually.

# A simplified content calendar

Creating and managing your content marketing initiatives can be tricky. Planning and being organised will make this important task more manageable.

A content calendar is a powerful and effective way of being proactive about your marketing goals. It can help you remain accountable to your content commitment and help you reassess – at any time – if your planned content is still relevant and consistent. How – and why – to write the best 'About' page for your website

We all expect the technical aspects of creating a website to be daunting. But what many entrepreneurs underestimate is just how hard it can be to get the content on your website right. When you only have a few minutes to impress new visitors, the words on your website aren't just words – they're your elevator pitch.

Here are our tried and tested tips for writing a great 'About' page.

# What is an 'About' page and why is it important?

An 'About' page is a designated page on your website where you tell visitors who you are, what you do, why you do it and a little about your business journey. When you're writing this page, keep in mind the visitors you're writing for – what do they want to know and why would they care? It's an important opportunity to connect with your audience by sharing your story.

## 1.  Include company details

Visitors to this page will be looking for specific information about you and your company. They want to know why they should do business with you, and choose you rather than one of your competitors. Only include information that is true and relevant. Be upfront about how long you've been in the industry and how you can solve their specific problem.

Also include details like:

- If your business is family-owned
- Your business values and what makes your company special
- Where you're based and what area(s) you service
- Your areas of expertise

## 2.  Stick to the facts

It can be easy to get carried away when you're writing this page but remember you want to sell your business, not oversell yourself. By being transparent, even if you're just starting out, your customers will learn that they can trust you and what you offer. Introduce your team or if you're a solo operation, share your passion and reason for existence – be relatable. Your unique story and business journey form part of your brand story.

## 3.  List credentials, awards and testimonials

If your company has won or been nominated for any certificates or awards, be sure to include them. This external validation can instill confidence in your prospective customers. If you have specific credentials or training, be sure to list them here too.

You can also include customer testimonials or any press coverage on your website – that way new visitors can read unbiased social proof of your service or products. Don't forget to add buttons that direct new visitors to your social media channels and if you have a newsletter, be sure to make the sign-up button clear and easy to find.

Writing your 'About' page is a great opportunity to remind yourself why you started your business – and why you're passionate about what you do. The goal is to convey these points to your customers in a succinct, meaningful way.

# Napkin notes:
# Crafting content

1.  A content strategy takes your brand story, combines it with content marketing, and produces something truly helpful for your customers.
2.  It's important to have a deep understanding of who your customers are so that you can offer them the content they need.
3.  A content calendar means you're strategic with what to share, when. It's a powerful and effective way of being proactive about your marketing goals.
4.  The 'About' page on your website is an important opportunity to connect with your audience by sharing your story.
5.  By being transparent, even if you're just starting out, your customers will learn that they can trust you and what you offer.

# 04

# Connecting with your customers

# How to connect with your customers to create a community

Being able to connect with your customers is an essential part of e-commerce. While you may not always be able to do so in person, there are still ways to make a connection – and foster brand loyalty – online. The goal is to turn your customers into brand advocates, by becoming invaluable to them. How do you do that? Here are a few ideas.

**Connected customers are repeat customers because they choose to be. And they're vital to the success of your business.**

## 1. Be personal and authentic

Your customers are real people, so address them that way. A one-size-fits-all approach doesn't work anymore – the needs of your customers vary. Figure out a way to segment your audience so you can focus on their particular needs, and speak to them in a way that resonates with them. Outline your customers' problems and how your product is the solution they need.

## 2. Ask for feedback – and use it

If you're not sure which problems your products solve for your customers, ask them. You can do this through customer surveys, polls or even on social media. Use these customer insights to make improvements where necessary.

But don' t just ask for feedback. Use it. If you don't listen to your customers, you'll give them the impression that you don't care about what they have to say.

> "You have to keep updated and know the nature of each platform. Each has their own culture and you need to respect that and have ways of managing interactions on each platform."

**See this advice come to life by scanning the QR code below.**

**Founder of clinimed.co.za**
Dr. Mathobela Matjekane

## 3. Engage your customers on social media

Social media marketing should go hand in hand with all your other marketing efforts. It's not enough to have a social media presence – you need to create and share engaging content. Build a community around the shared interests your brand and customers have.

If you're not sure how, pretend you're having a real-life conversation. Don't type what you wouldn't say: make it natural. Include captions on your posts so your readers have more context around what you're sharing and why. Ask them questions, and encourage your audience to give their input.

## 4. Email marketing

No one needs more unnecessary emails – the internet is already filled with so much information. If you're going to send your customers an email, it needs to cut through the clutter. How are you going to do that? By being helpful.

Before sending out an email newsletter, ask yourself:

- What does my email offer that customers can't get elsewhere?
- Can I make my message more succinct?
- Are my emails mobile-friendly? The latest stats show that more than 75% of traffic is on mobile devices.

# 5. Interact using webinars

Some businesses prefer to network in person, but this isn't always possible. There's a good second-best option, though – webinars. These are a great marketing tool for creating 'real-life' communication. Record the sessions and share them on social media, so that even if your audience can't attend in real-time, your webinar lives on.

Remember that webinars aren't new, though, so there will have to be something special about yours. It should be relevant and interesting to stand out from the crowd. To harness the power of this tool, make sure it makes your audiences' lives easier or more interesting. You could share industry tips and tricks, conduct interviews or host an FAQ session.

Webinars drive engagement because they're interactive. By using the chat feature, your audience can feel part of the conversation, and your community.

# 6. Contribute to guest posts

Guest posts are an effective way of increasing your brand's reach. They also build trust. When other businesses or influencers publish your content, they're endorsing it. If your content is of real value to these audiences, they'll come to trust you as an expert.

Before you start guest blogging, make sure it forms part of your content strategy. Also, include specific goals, like:

- More website traffic
- Increased brand awareness
- Positioning yourself or your brand as a subject matter expert in your niche

Another reason to consider guest blogging is SEO. A backlink (a link from another website) from a successful website has major SEO benefits. It also strengthens your domain's authority which helps to improve your website's position in search results.

## 7. Podcasts and videos

Did you know that podcasts appear in Google search results? And that Google indexes transcripts? Google Podcasts lets you "find and listen to the world's podcasts for free." This means, if you have a podcast, it'll show up in search results you couldn't access before. This is great for SEO and could open your brand up to a new audience.

Similarly, videos for YouTube or Facebook can be a great way to connect with your customers. Do you have knowledge that could help your customers? Create short videos to upload onto YouTube or Facebook. Think tutorials, webinars or DIY videos. This can be helpful if you offer a service that can be difficult to understand.

For a more dynamic approach, you could use Facebook Live or Instagram Live videos. These work well for restaurants, venues, or small businesses that manufacture on site. Invite customers into your space for a few minutes, or share 'secrets of the trade' they wouldn't be able to see otherwise. Everyone loves a behind-the-scenes peek.

Connecting with your customers is one of the golden rules of content marketing. Luckily, you now have the tools to do just that.

# Email marketing: the basics

Email marketing, in theory, is pretty simple. It's a marketing tool used to build – and maintain – relationships with customers, keeping them updated on new products or services and the value they could offer. It's a great way to promote connection and increase your community.

"The big thing about email marketing is that it's the last piece of technology that's completely agnostic. Unlike social media where you don't own your community, the platform does. With an email database, you do own it, your list is your list. You have full control over it."

**See this advice come to life by scanning the QR code below.**

**VP of Digital Strategy**
**at sitecare.com**
Jason Bagley

Email marketing is also about 'owning' this valuable data. If you've built up your community on Facebook, what would you do if the platform shut down tomorrow? How would customers know where to find you or which solutions you offer to solve their problems?

# Email marketing is a great way to promote connection and increase your community.

Email marketing includes newsletters, product news, event invites and education campaigns. If you don't already use email marketing as one of your marketing strategies, you should think about it. It's an effective way to build relationships with your customers, and when done correctly, it can keep your customers engaged with your brand, serving as a reminder of why they should continue to buy your products or use your service.

# Email marketing dos and don'ts:

But there are, obviously, good and bad sides to email marketing. Here are the most important dos and don'ts.

## Do:

### Implement double opt-ins

Even when customers have subscribed to your newsletter, you need to make sure it was done on purpose. One way to do this is to send a confirmation email afterwards, asking them to verify their consent. If you use email marketing software, you can set this up to send automatically.

### Be responsible with personal information

While it may seem fairly harmless, when you're building a mailing list, you're gathering and storing your customers' personal information. And with this comes the responsibility to process this data responsibly, following the POPI (Protection of Personal Information) Act.

## Don't:

### Buy mailing lists

Cutting corners will cost you. While it may be tempting to buy mailing lists to increase your reach, it's illegal to send unsolicited emails to customers who have not opted-in to receive them. Over and above this, you're bound to be marked as spam by the customers who are receiving your emails against their will.

### Try to cross-sell

It's a lazy assumption to make that customers who have signed up for one of your product newsletters are automatically interested in all of your other newsletters or brand mailers. In fact, according to the POPI Act, you're only legally allowed to send commercial emails to customers who have given explicit permission for you to do so. You could even be asked to provide proof of this, so it's not worth risking.

### Hide the option to unsubscribe

To avoid being flagged as a spammer, ensure that you include an 'unsubscribe' link in the body of your email – preferably somewhere easily accessible. Once this link has been clicked, the email address must be immediately removed from your mailing list. Don't make customers have to provide a lengthy reason or have to confirm via another email.

We all receive many emails every day, the last thing we need is unsolicited ones. Remember that even when someone has signed up for your newsletter, your email is one of many they'll receive that day. So make it worth reading.

## How do you get your email to stand out from the crowd?

1.  Make sure your email is unique – tell your audience something they don't already know or in a way they're not used to or don't expect.
2.  Be short and snappy – get to the point as soon as possible.
3.  Make sure your email looks good on mobile and in different email programmes. You can use tools like Litmus to do this easily.

Tell your audience something they don't already know or in a way they're not used to or don't expect.

**The power of mobile friendly**

Did you know?
According to Statista, as of January 2021, there were 38.13 million active internet users in South Africa. Among them, an overwhelming majority (more than 36 million) used mobile internet.

## Get the basics right

Email marketing is a big part of your online brand. So make it visually appealing. Avoid any mistakes or typos slipping through the cracks by sending yourself a test mail and thoroughly checking every detail (including links!) before sending these emails to customers.

An easy email win is to personalise your message. If you know your customers' names, address them directly.

There are many popular email marketing platforms available, some of which include free options. These are ideal if you're a start-up or you don't have a big budget for your marketing efforts. Examples are MailChimp, Campaign Monitor and ConvertKit.

## How to write – and measure – email subject lines

The subject line of your email is the first thing your audience sees – so it needs to be interesting enough to open. But how will you know if you're getting it right? You can track the success of your email subject lines by looking at the data. According to Campaign Monitor, an average email open rate should be between 15 to 25%, an average click-through rate should be 2.5% and you're looking for a click-to-open rate of 20 to 30%.

- An email open rate is the percentage of your audience that decided to open your email.
- A click-through rate is the percentage of your audience that clicked on a link or a button once they opened your email.
- And finally, the click-to-open rate is the percentage of unique clicks compared to the unique opens. Out of every person that opened your email, how many of those readers stuck around to engage and read it?

If you're using a tool like Mailchimp or Campaign Monitor, these stats will be available to you in a dashboard.

# 1. Make sure your subject line is short and to the point

Your email subject line needs to be a short, interesting summary of what your email is about and why customers should take time out of their busy day to read it. This is probably the most important part of your email.

Interestingly enough, stats show that subject lines of 6-10 words are more likely to be opened than those with 21 or more. If you're boring your readers in the subject line, they're not going to be enticed to carry on reading.

# 2. Add some urgency – if there is some

The aim here is to gently persuade your audience to read your email now, in case they forget to do it later. Use words like 'now', 'today', 'don't miss out'. But don't try to fool your readers. If you do, they'll remember it next time and scroll past your email. Or worse, unsubscribe from them altogether.

# 3. Be warm and friendly

Use simple, approachable language in your subject line and throughout your email. And, if it's suited to your brand, consider using emojis as well. But not too many! One or two is plenty.

In short, when sending emails to your customers, make sure you're telling a story worth reading. Send high-quality emails that boost your brand's reputation and add genuine value to your customers' lives. Make sure your email copy is relatable, interesting and appeals to your audience's emotions. Engage with them: they're real people and they're more interested in emails from real people too.

# How to choose the right social media platforms for your business

Once your website is up and running, you'll probably be ready to venture into the world of social media! But where to start? Your social media marketing should go hand in hand with your content strategy and all your other marketing efforts. By harnessing the right social media platforms, you can distribute your content widely – increasing your brand awareness and, hopefully, your sales too.

The most popular social media channels at the moment are Facebook, Twitter, Instagram, TikTok, YouTube, Pinterest and LinkedIn. While it's possible to have a presence on each of them, it's better to master one or two at a time.

**Focusing your social media efforts will guarantee a better return on your investment.**

## What to consider

Some of the considerations you'll need to keep in mind when choosing which social media platform to focus on are:

- What are your specific social media goals?
- Which platforms are your customers using?
- Which platforms are you comfortable using, or do your team members have experience in?
- Which platforms are your competitors using? If you're not sure, do a quick competitor review to find out what's working for them.
- Which platform is best suited for the type of content you intend to post? If you have a lot of great images, consider using a platform like Instagram or Pinterest. If your content isn't as visually strong, consider another platform like Twitter or Facebook.

One more question to consider is how you will know if your efforts are working. Traffic and conversions measure the success of your social media – you'll need to set realistic social media marketing goals and measure them regularly. You can measure how much web traffic comes from each platform to determine if one platform is performing better than the other. And then double down on that one!

## Know who your audience is

To create meaningful content on social media, it's essential to identify your audience – the more specific you are, the easier it will be to narrow your focus. Here are some guiding questions to help you get started:

- Who are your customers?
- What are their specific characteristics? Things like their age, gender, etc.
- What devices do they use to access your website? (You can get this information quite simply from Google Analytics.)
- Other than your product/service, what else are your potential customers interested in?

The answers to these questions will help you create a general profile of your customer base.

## Explore the platforms your customers use

Now that you know who you're targeting, and what you'd like to achieve by using social media, you need to determine which platforms are best suited to your business. Your customers may be on multiple platforms but this doesn't mean you need to be on all of them as well. Rather focus your attention on one or two platforms, and do them well.

Unless you work on it full time, it's not possible to be present on all of the available social media platforms without compromising on the quality of your content. Also, remember that there's a difference between presence and engagement.

Engagement means how much your customers interact with the content you're sharing: the number of page likes, comments and shares. Your customers may be on Facebook, but they may interact more (and be driven to make purchases) via Instagram, for example.

Engagement means how much your customers interact with the content you're sharing: the number of page likes, comments and shares.

Social media success relies on testing and iterating. Adjust your posting schedule and content once you see when your customers are most engaged – Google Analytics can help you uncover when your site is the busiest, and you'll be able to get insights on post performance from each social media platform.

**Conversion tip**
Remember: if you want to drive sales, make sure your customers land on your product page or sign up page directly from your social media posts. Make their journey as seamless as possible.

## Understand where your content fits best

Your content goals will not be suitable for every platform. Here's a quick cheat sheet of what content fits where.

### Facebook

- With over 2.45 billion users, it's no surprise that Facebook remains at the top of the list of social media platforms.
- Facebook is great for developing your brand identity, broadening your reach, creating a community and keeping customers informed of changes.

### Twitter

- Twitter is a popular choice for many businesses and is popular among readers who want to keep up with the world but don't want to read long-form content.
- Twitter uses hashtags (organising content according to a certain word or phrase), making this platform ideal for real-time updates and promoting events.

## Pinterest

- According to Statista, more than 47% of Pinterest users log on specifically to make a purchase.
- As Pinterest is entirely visual, you'll need high-quality imagery to get the best results from this platform.
- Pinterest is predominantly used by women, so if your business is female-focused, this channel could be an ideal platform for you.

## YouTube

- YouTube is considered the second most popular search engine after Google.
- One billion people visit YouTube each month globally, with 100 hours of video uploaded every 60 seconds. That's a lot of traffic you can reach.
- Cisco reports that by 2022, online video will make up more than 82% of all consumer internet traffic, so this is a trend to get involved in now. Viewers of your content have the option to share your videos on their social media platforms. They can also comment on your videos, making it a valuable way to connect with your (potential) customers.

## LinkedIn

- LinkedIn is ideal for creating a professional business network community.
- Having a LinkedIn profile helps build business credibility and is a valuable marketing tool to have at your disposal.
- LinkedIn enables you to interact with like-minded professionals and other industry experts.
- Due to the unique focus of LinkedIn, this platform is best used for business-to-business (B2B) lead generation, recruiting and networking.

## Instagram

Like Pinterest, Instagram is dependent on appealing, good-quality imagery.

- Instagram promises 'less noise' than Facebook and relies on imagery for lead generation (sales). By adding buttons to your posts, or using the 'swipe up' feature in your stories when you have enough followers, you can easily take your customers from viewing your products to purchasing them.
- Consider using Instagram for lead generation, creating a community, expanding your reach or affirming your brand identity.

> "Ask yourself: if someone else had to say to their friend, "Hey, have you seen the _ account on Instagram?" What would they say? If you can't articulate it, as clearly as that, in a simple sentence, then your promise is wishy-washy."

See this advice come to life by scanning the QR code below.

**Founder @SouthAfrica**
Craig Rodney

## TikTok

- TikTok encourages users to upload short videos, focused on users under 30 years of age.
- To use TikTok for marketing, you can create your own channel and share relevant videos.
- You can work with influencers to spread your content to a broader audience.
- Create a specific hashtag for your business and encourage your customers to use it whenever they post about your products.
- Consider advertising on TikTok. While the platform is still in its infancy for this purpose, TikTok shows great potential for growth as a platform.

No matter the platform you choose, every small business needs a social media presence of some description. But before you dive into the deep pool of social media, it's important to understand where your potential customers already are and join them on those platforms. Choose one or two of the best-suited platforms for your business, and focus on doing them well.

# A helpful guide to Instagram for business

With more than one billion active monthly users, Instagram is one of the most powerful social media marketing platforms. Luckily, Instagram is relatively easy to use, even for beginners. It's also packed with helpful features and functionality that you can use to promote your brand and expand your reach.

## The benefits of Instagram for business

Instagram enables businesses of all sizes to grow their audiences, increase brand awareness, and generate more sales. Instagram reports that 90% of the app's users follow at least one business. In addition, nearly 85% of Instagram users use this platform to find new products or solutions.

You can use Instagram to promote products and services, share relevant company-related news and updates, and communicate with your target audience. Plus, it's free to use (unless you want to pay to advertise). This platform also offers various ways to share content, including Instagram Stories, IGTV, and regular feed posts.

90% of Instagram users follow at least one business account. In addition, nearly 85% of them use the platform to find new products or solutions.

# How to get started with Instagram for business

If you already have a personal Instagram account, you can easily switch to a business profile (just go to Settings > Switch to Professional Account).

If you don't have an account or your existing one is unrelated to your business, you can create a new profile. An Instagram Business account has added functionality that a personal account doesn't, such as:

- Additional messaging features, including Call To Action (CTA) buttons
- Instagram Insights, which gives you insight into your followers and post engagement
- A paid ads feature that leverages Facebook's optimised ad delivery system
- Access to the Instagram Shopping feature that turns your profile into an online storefront

Once you set up an Instagram account, you'll be ready to create and optimise your page. There are a few important factors to consider upfront, like your:

### Profile picture

Most brands use their logos. Ideally, the image will be 110 x 110 pixels and align with what you use on other platforms, including your website and other social media profiles.

### Bio

With a 150-character limit, you should use this space to quickly and concisely communicate who you are and what you do. Consider using emojis, hashtags (which are clickable), and line breaks.

### Website URL

You can update this URL as often as you want. For example, you can link to a specific landing page if you're running a promotion.

You can also add your email, phone number, and physical address. Instagram will create corresponding CTA buttons.

**Best practices when using Instagram for business**

Once you have your business profile set up, you can use it to promote your brand. Here are some of the best practices to keep in mind:

1. Focus on creating high-quality, visual content
2. Post consistently
3. Use clear CTAs
4. Encourage engagement

# Focus on creating high-quality, visual content

Instagram is all about the visuals. To stand out from the crowd, you'll need to make sure your posts are aesthetically pleasing and align with your brand identity.

Instagram provides lots of built-in features, including filters, overlays, and special effects, but you can also use third-party tools that offer pre-made post templates.

# Post consistently

If you're familiar with content marketing, you probably already understand the importance of posting regularly. A consistent posting schedule can help keep your audience engaged and interested.

To determine the best days and times to post, we recommend using Instagram Insights. You can also learn about your audience's demographics and find out when they're most active. To save yourself the manual work of posting, you can use a scheduling tool.

# Use clear CTAs

Any action you want your audience to take needs to be clear and simple – and should stand out. In post captions, you can't link directly to a website but you can direct your visitors to click on CTA buttons and links on your profile:

Once you reach 10 000 followers, you'll be able to include 'Swipe Up' links in your Stories.

# Encourage engagement

Creating an engaged Instagram community can help you gain more followers and maintain interest among your audience. To encourage engagement, always tag people and pages that you mention.

Using relevant hashtags is also an effective way to position your posts among users who are interested in related topics. You don't want to go overboard, though. We recommend between one and three per post, included in the caption.

**To encourage engagement, always tag people and pages that you mention.**

It's a good idea to develop a strategy for managing comments. You might respond to every comment to increase trust and engagement, or only questions. Either way, aim to reply promptly to demonstrate strong customer service.

# Use Instagram to expand your business

There are many different social media platforms out there, so deciding between them can be difficult. If you want to access a vast audience and you have visually engaging content to share, Instagram is hard to beat.

# A helpful guide to LinkedIn for business

LinkedIn reports that over 660 million people use the website to grow their businesses, expand their professional networks, or look for better employment opportunities. If you're one of them, understanding how to get the most out of this platform can often lead to exciting career developments.

Not sure where to start? Don't worry, even a few minor changes to the way you use LinkedIn could make a big difference. We've outlined a few easy ways to get the most out of this platform.

## The benefits of LinkedIn for business

Before we get into the best way to use LinkedIn, let's discuss why it's important to have a presence on this platform in the first place. LinkedIn gives you:

- A platform to showcase what your business does, and post updates to those interested in your field.
- The ability to follow what colleagues and experts in your field are interested in.
- A platform to make connections with others in your industry.

In 2021, social media is key to professional networking, and LinkedIn is one of the most effective platforms for this purpose. On average, each connection you make on LinkedIn expands your potential network by about 400 people – and dozens of relevant networking opportunities.

Did you know? Each new connection expands your potential network by 400 people.

# 3 effective ways to get the most out of LinkedIn

Many people set up LinkedIn accounts and then forget about them. While it's possible to luck your way into networking opportunities just by having a profile, it's highly unlikely. To take advantage of your network, you have to maintain an active presence.

## 1.  Focus on content

The best way to grow your LinkedIn network is by sharing content related to your industry. You can post articles that you find interesting, or share your thoughts. It's also a great place to engage in discussions with people who take the time to interact with your content.

LinkedIn can also form part of your content marketing strategy. It's one of the few social media platforms well-suited to long-form posts.

## 2.  Optimise your posts for reach and impact

Sharing posts is a start, but you have to work to make sure they don't go unnoticed. Optimise your LinkedIn content by:

Following a posting schedule.

Sharing content consistently will grow your network and set you up to one day be seen as an expert. Gauge when your LinkedIn community is most active and publish your posts then.

Adding relevant hashtags to each new post.

This makes it easier for people outside of your network to find your content, which can increase your chances for worthwhile connections.

Keeping captions short and sharp.

Include simple CTAs that direct your connections to what you'd like them to do next.

Tagging people and pages when you mention them.

LinkedIn will notify them, bringing relevant connections to your post.

Just like other social media platforms, your content has to compete for attention as users scroll through their feeds. These best practices will help your posts stand out.

### 3. Encourage engagement

Creating engaging LinkedIn posts can be a challenge, which is what makes captions so important. Use them to feature interesting quotes from your content or pose questions that encourage readers to interact. You'll need someone to respond to user engagement promptly so your followers don't lose interest in engaging with you. Think of it as a conversation that you're having online: if two days pass between comments, the conversation will fall flat.

"It's got to start with what it is that makes you unique, what your offering is. From there, do the work: relentless interaction."

**See this advice come to life by scanning the QR code below.**

**Singer and Songwriter**
Zolani Mahola

Finally, consider using LinkedIn polls to gather feedback and boost engagement. This can be particularly helpful for learning about emerging trends in your field or conducting consumer research.

As with most things in life, the more you put into LinkedIn, the more you'll get out of it. If your business becomes known for sharing relevant, engaging content and updates, you'll soon attract a dedicated following that can help you network your way to opportunities.

# A helpful guide to Facebook and Twitter for business

The right social media platforms are the ones your customers (and potential customers) are on. Let's explore the unique benefits Facebook and Twitter provide for growing your business and discuss how best to leverage these platforms to increase your brand's visibility.

## The benefits of using Facebook and Twitter for business

Facebook users spend an average of 38 minutes a day browsing the platform. Once you get customers to follow your page, you'll be able to remind them of your brand each time you post new content. Depending on your business, you can also use this platform to collect leads or offer customer support.

Twitter's user base is not as big as Facebook's, with 192 million daily active users compared to the latter's 1.84 billion. However, Twitter still has its place online. If you're publishing short and engaging content, Twitter is ideal.

Despite its smaller audience, Twitter users are often more engaged, which makes it a valuable channel for businesses looking to increase brand loyalty.

**5 Tips for using Facebook and Twitter for business**
Once you have your business profile set up, you can use it to promote your brand. Here are some of the best practices to keep in mind:

1.  Choose the right type of account
2.  Focus on quality content
3.  Use hashtags sparingly and keep your copy short
4.  Respond to comments quickly
5.  Set a posting schedule

# 1. Choose the right type of account

Some social media platforms offer special accounts for businesses. Often, they have access to additional features that regular users don't, such as analytics, marketing tools, online shopping functionality, and more.

For example, Facebook for business offers specialised functionality depending on the type of industry you're in. You can even set up a Stores page that shows all of your locations.

Twitter, on the other hand, doesn't offer these specialised business profiles. You'd need to sign up for a regular account, with access to the same tools as everyone else.

# 2. Focus on quality content

As a rule of thumb, 80 to 90% of the content you publish on your business's social media accounts should be fun, engaging, or informative rather than pushing sales. These might not transform directly into sales, but they do foster engagement. Followers are more likely to interact with your profiles if they see your brand as fun as interesting. As a result, the 10 to 20% of your social content that does focus on sales and promotions will have a much better reception.

# 3. Use hashtags sparingly and keep your copy short

Use one or two relevant hashtags on each of your posts so that your content reaches the right audience. To grab their attention, your copy should be short and to the point. To increase your engagement, accompany your posts with images and captions with quotes or key takeaways.

If your strategy is to share many articles and blog posts from your website, Facebook is the better platform as it enables you to include longer descriptions. Twitter, on the other hand, is ideal if you want to share short snippets of information or business news.

## 4.  Respond to comments quickly

One of the best ways to foster engagement on social media is to answer comments left on your posts. If users see that they can interact with you, they're much more likely to keep doing so.

That process works much the same whether you're using Twitter or Facebook. However, Facebook also enables customers to leave reviews, which gives you an additional channel to engage with customers.

As a rule of thumb, if you receive a bad review, it's best to reply and offer to fix the customer's problem. This demonstrates your willingness to correct mistakes and provide quality service.

## 5.  Set a posting schedule

Finally, remember that users on each social media platform are most active during specific times. On Facebook, followers are more likely to see your content around midday, and posts that go live on Wednesdays receive the most engagement.

When it comes to Twitter, activity peaks earlier in the morning on Wednesdays and Fridays. You can use this information to help you decide when to publish new content. A posting schedule or content calendar is one key aspect of a comprehensive content strategy.

## Leverage Facebook and Twitter to grow your business

Social media can be a powerful tool for businesses to engage their customers without being too intrusive. It's a must-have marketing channel for modern brands – as long as you approach it in the right way, and remember that you're speaking to real humans.

# Napkin notes:
# Connecting with your customers

1. Being able to connect with your customers is an essential part of e-commerce.
2. Email marketing can be used to build a community, allowing you to connect with customers, keeping them engaged in your product and service developments.
3. Your social media marketing should go hand in hand with your content strategy and all your other marketing efforts. You don't have to be on every social media platform, but you do need to focus on the ones you are on.
4. Whichever social media platform you choose, it's important to encourage engagement by responding to comments quickly, and posting regularly.
5. As a rule of thumb, 80 to 90% of the content you publish on your business's social media accounts should be fun, engaging, or informative rather than pushing sales.

# 05

# Understanding SEO

# The essentials of SEO

SEO can seem like a foreign language if you don't understand it. But as a small business owner, it's a language you need to learn. Search engine optimisation, or SEO, is the process of improving your website so that search engines, like Google, can find your content and display it as a suggested search result to the right audience. The goal? To make it easier for prospective customers to find you – and choose to use you.

## SEO takes time

Ranking as a top result in Google doesn't happen overnight. First, you need an SEO strategy. Identify the keywords or phrases that your target market uses when searching for your product or service, and then optimise your content so that it ranks well for those searches.

Be careful not to overload your content with keywords just for the sake of it – you want to optimise your content for your readers first, search engines second.

SEO is essential whether you're already established or a new start-up, because it generates traffic to your website. An increase in traffic to your website helps with conversions, which helps with profit. Win-win!

Not sure where to start? Here are some essential tips.

**5 essential SEO tips**
1. Focus on technical SEO
2. Focus on local SEO
3. Prioritise content creation
4. Leverage social media
5. Use backlinks

# Focus on technical SEO

Technical SEO is the process of optimising your website so that it's easy for search engine 'crawlers' (the little bots) to read and index your website. They do this constantly, noting website changes or broken links, like a 404 (page not found) error. Ideally, you want this process to be quick and simple for the crawler. Even if your content is the best out there, technical issues can affect how it is found and indexed. Security is also important – make sure your hosting provider offers SSL/TLS certificates.

You don't need a technical background to improve your technical SEO – you can still make improvements:

- Use a plugin like Yoast to create a sitemap and submit it to Google.
- Fix any performance issues. A slow-loading website will affect your website's chances of performing well in search engines.
- Ensure you're using a reputable web hosting provider and, if you are using WordPress, consider performance improving plugins.
- Make sure your website works across various devices and screen sizes. Websites that are not mobile-friendly will not be ranked highly.
- Fix any old or broken links – search engines will downgrade your content if you send your readers to too many dead ends.
- Optimise your images – they should be relevant and appropriately captioned.

# Focus on local SEO

Almost a third of mobile searches are location-based. Even if your potential customers don't specify their location, Google automatically prioritises results according to location.

Here are some simple ways to make use of this opportunity:

- Include information on your site that shows you operate locally, such as your physical address and location-specific keywords.
- Create a Google My Business profile to give your business an extra presence on the search results page.
- Add your website to local listing sites.
- Use Structured Data like reviews and events, where applicable.

# Prioritise content creation

The best way to write content for new prospective customers is to know what they're already searching for. If you're not sure, there are plenty of tools you can use to define the keywords that relate to your business.

But your content is not just for SEO – it has to be genuinely engaging and interesting to your audience. Your content should incorporate target keywords organically – do not force the use of keywords by compromising your content. The structure is important too: make sure your content is easily readable by using page titles and headlines.

While content marketing does take time and effort, it's a vital tool in forming a relationship with your website visitors.

# Leverage social media

Social media goes hand in hand with your content creation strategy: you can use your social media channels to distribute your content widely. By sharing your content this way, you're increasing your content exposure. When you write helpful, relevant content, your readers are also more likely to share it on their networks. This authentic social proof is priceless.

# Use backlinks

A backlink is when another website posts a link to your website in its content. When other sites refer their visitors to your website, it improves your position in search engines. Quality backlinks mean your content is worth reading. While this may happen organically, you can also implement an outreach strategy where you reach out to your contacts and request that they incorporate a relevant link to your content.

In essence, remember that while SEO is for search engines, your website content is for real people. Make sure your content is optimised for them first.

# 3 essential tips for your SEO marketing strategy

Many responsibilities come along with starting your own business. One of the most important tasks is to make your website highly visible online so that customers can easily find you. Fortunately, there are simple SEO techniques you can use to promote your site on search engines like Google. Applying a few key tactics when creating content can go a long way.

## Why SEO matters

Optimising your content is necessary if you hope to get your website in the top results on search engines like Google. This can drive new traffic to your business. The top Google search result gets over 42% of traffic, the second result gets only about 12%, and the rest of the results fall below 9%.

Effective SEO requires a careful balance. It's important to use the right terms that allow search engines to know what your content is about, while not overloading your site content with keywords and making it unreadable.

What's more, 51% of web traffic is 'organic', meaning visitors find your site through online searches. Organic traffic, unlike paid advertising, is completely free. This makes SEO a cost-effective marketing method.

> The top Google search result gets over 42% of traffic, the second result gets only about 12%, and the rest of the results fall below 9%.

# 3 essential SEO tips for every entrepreneur

If you want to spread the word about your business and attract more visitors, you'll need to incorporate SEO into your site management process. Let's look at three ways to do that.

## 1. Incorporate on-site and technical SEO to improve your content

On-site or on-page SEO refers to techniques used to optimise your content. This primarily means using keywords in your posts, titles, headings, and URLs.

However, you should also pay attention to technical aspects of your website that impact your search engine rankings, such as loading speed and mobile responsiveness.

Making sure your website stays fast by regularly testing it with Google PageSpeed Insights is wise. It's also important that your site is viewable on smartphones as well as desktops, so make sure to implement responsive design.

In general terms, about 20% of your SEO efforts should be focused in this direction. Many tools can help, including Google's Keyword Planner and several WordPress plugins.

## 2. Use content marketing to rank higher and attract visitors

Content marketing is the process of creating authoritative, relevant, and unique content to attract visitors. This should make up the bulk of your SEO efforts.

You can distribute content via multiple channels, such as a blog, social media accounts, or even email. Thoughtful, informative content that provides value to your target market has a strong chance to rank well with search engines and draw customers to your site.

## 3. Implement off-site SEO to make connections across the web

Finally, off-site SEO consists of practices that affect content outside your website. Key off-site strategies include:

- **Link building:** Encouraging links across the web that lead back to your site.
- **Guest posts:** Writing posts for other websites' blogs.
- **Social media:** Promoting your business and website on various social networks.

These practices point users from around the web towards your site, to generate more traffic. Links to your content from other high-quality sites can go a long way towards boosting your visibility and even improving your search engine rankings.

## Getting started with SEO

As you can see, there's a lot that goes into optimising your website for search engines. Understanding SEO is a critical part of any e-commerce store's success. With these tips, and some dedicated time, you'll be well on your way to SEO success.

# A quick guide to conducting an SEO Audit

SEO is like a key that opens up your website to search engines such as Google . Technically, SEO is the practice of making your website and its content appealing to search engine algorithms. Every small business should have an SEO marketing strategy of some sort. Why? Not only is SEO traffic (visitors to your website because of SEO) free of charge, but if you create the right content you can grow long-term, sustainable traffic. It also helps build trust and credibility for your business.

So what is an SEO audit? An SEO audit is a review of your website looking for any evidence of 'best practices' that could make your site more attractive to search engines. A quick audit will ensure you're not losing out on any potential traffic and customers.

It might seem like SEO is a lot of work – it is. But it's an ongoing investment, well worth the time and energy. Here's how to conduct an SEO audit on your site.

## Choose the right tools

There are plenty of free and paid-for tools to help you with various aspects of an SEO audit. The two essentials are Google Analytics and Google Search Console.

**Google Analytics can tell you:**

- How much organic traffic your website gets: organic traffic is unpaid traffic. Visitors find your site by searching for a keyword and clicking on a link.
- Which pages receive the most organic traffic.
- Visitor engagement (bounce rate, time spent on your site, and more) for organic traffic.
- Organic traffic conversion information: which of those visitors are 'converting' and leading to a specific action: more sales or business, or signing up for more info.

**Google Search Console is helpful because it:**

- Provides details on how your site is performing in Google search results, including what search queries your website shows up for.
- Submits sitemaps to Google. A sitemap is a structured list of the pages on your website. They are used for search engines to make sense of your site.
- Picks up errors and other issues with your website.
- Lets Google communicate any problems with your website directly to you.

Both Google Analytics and Google Search Console are free to use and will lead you through the step-by-step process to start using them with your site.

# Check for missing pages

One of the most helpful things about Google Search Console is that it will let you know if you have any missing pages on your site. Missing pages are links that result in a 404 (or page not found) error. You can also use a tool like Screaming Frog to scan your website. It performs a crawl of your site and points out any 404 errors that you can fix. There's a free version of this tool that can scan up to 500 pages.

# Make sure your site is mobile-friendly

It's no surprise that mobile-friendly is a must today, especially in South Africa where over 70% of users are looking at websites from their mobile devices. Google has adopted a mobile-first algorithm, so having a site that isn't mobile-friendly is costly – it will lose you search engine traffic. You can use a tool like Google's Mobile-Friendly Testing Tool to find out how your site is doing, and how to fix any issues it identifies.

Over 70% of South African users are looking at websites from their mobile phones.

# Check website performance

If you want your site to perform well in search engines, page load time is critical. Slow load times can be a result of poor coding or a slow hosting provider, or because your pages or images are too big. You can use a plugin to reduce page load speed.

**Measuring site performance**

There are a few tools you can use to measure site performance, including:

- PageSpeed Insights
- WebPageTest.org

You'll need to test a few pages, as these tools test individual pages. What's helpful is that they provide insight into how to fix the issues. Choosing a reputable hosting provider is also really important for website performance.

# Review your content

Content is an integral part of good SEO. It's important to have a plan of action for any content you produce on your website (blog posts, product pages etc). Make sure the content is written around topics central to the products and services you provide – not around single keywords. The goal with all content is for it to be helpful, well written and provide value to the people who will read it.

To find out which pages perform well in search engines, you can use Google Analytics and Google Search Console.

### Google Analytics:

Top-performing pages

Look at the report on top-performing landing pages to see organic traffic.

Page views and engagement

Look at page views and engagement to determine which of your content is most successful. Engagement metrics are things like how long people stay on the page, and how likely they are to 'bounce' – to leave immediately afterwards.

**Google Search Console:**

Search Engine Performance

Look at your Search Engine Performance report to find which pages get the most impressions and clicks.

No duplicate content

Look for any duplicate content. Help Google take the guesswork out of figuring which page should rank for a keyword and make sure the content on your website is unique and to the point.

No thin or irrelevant content

Thin or irrelevant content could be pages that offer little value – category pages, author pages and pagination links that create a lot of extra work for search engines to crawl. If you remove these pages, the search engines can focus on the important pages.

Improve low value pages

To find out which are your lowest value pages, use the Site Content Report from Google Analytics to find pages with only a handful of views. If you have an important page with low page views, think about ways to improve this page's visibility by adding to the content and linking to it internally and externally.

Look for opportunities

If you have a high click-through rate but low impressions, you could improve the page's quality and ranking, and then see a big increase in traffic.

The goal with all content is for it to be helpful, well written and provide value to the people who will read it.

# Review your backlinks

Backlinks are links to your website from another website and form the cornerstone of any SEO campaign. Quality overrides quantity when it comes to backlinks. You can use the Links report in Google Search Console to find out which backlinks are linking to which pages, and the anchor text (with the link) that is being used. If you don't have many backlinks, there are a few things you can do.

- Check to see if your important pages are getting backlinks. If not, consider ways to secure backlinks to these pages. Also, check to see that backlinks are spread evenly across your site. For example, only having backlinks to the homepage is not a good distribution of links.
- Consider paid-for tools such as Ahrefs or Moz to determine the quality of the backlinks and check how your competitors are doing.
- Bad backlinks (links from spam or other unreliable sites) can be detrimental to your site's SEO performance. There are tools on Google Search Console to discredit these links.

# Use HTTPS

Finally, ensuring your website is secure is an essential part of your SEO strategy. Make sure your site is using an SSL certificate (identified by https in the website address). Google's SEO guidelines strongly suggest an SSL certificate, and all xneelo web hosting accounts include a free SSL certificate via LetsEncrypt. This ensures peace of mind for your visitors while contributing to your SEO ranking.

Building your website and adding the content is the hard work. Now that you've done that, you just have to ensure that you have the right SEO tools in place for search engines to be able to find that content – and show it to the visitors you need to reach.

# Napkin notes:
# Understanding SEO

1. There are plenty of free and paid-for tools to help you with various aspects of SEO.
2. Effective SEO requires a careful balance. It's important to use the right terms that allow search engines to know what your content is about, while not overloading your site content with keywords and making it unreadable.
3. Identify the keywords or phrases that your target market uses when searching for your product or service, and then optimise your content so that it ranks well for those searches.
4. If you want your site to perform well in search engines, page load time is critical.
5. It's no surprise that mobile-friendly is a must today, especially in South Africa where more than 70% of users are looking at websites from their mobile devices.

# 06

# Growing your online business

# What you need to know to start an online store

Starting an online store may seem like an intimidating process. But the barrier to entry for becoming an online retailer is actually quite low. That's because e-commerce platforms enable you to quickly and easily set up shop on the web – even if you've never done it before.

> "There's not really much to be afraid of these days (when starting an e-commerce business). More than ever, there are specialist providers, ready to support you every step of the way."

**See this advice come to life by scanning the QR code below.**

**Founder of payfast.co.za**
Jonathan Smit

## Hosting your e-commerce site

To set up an online store, you'll need a website listing your products for sale. The three key elements you'll require at this stage are a registered domain name, a hosting account, and an HTTPS connection (essential e-commerce security).

First on the list: your domain name. This acts as your site's address and makes it possible for customers to find and browse your store.

Next up, your hosting provider will manage the server where your website is stored. It's important to choose a provider that you're comfortable working with on a long-term basis because this will be an ongoing relationship. Before choosing a hosting company, you might want to test out each option's customer service. You'll want to look for 24/7 availability, quick responses to your queries, and clear explanations.

## Essential e-commerce security

E-commerce involves asking customers to trust you with sensitive information, including their credit card details. SSL (Secure Sockets Layer) certificates enable HTTPS, a secure connection between web browsers and your site's server, so your customers' information isn't likely to be stolen.

Of course, additional security measures can further protect your customers by preventing attacks and hackers. For instance, you may consider adding a Web Application Firewall (WAF) to your site. This helps to maintain your store's reputation as a safe place to shop online, and protects both your brand and revenue streams.

**South African e-commerce is expected to grow almost 9% annually over the next five years.**

## Choosing your e-commerce platform

Now that you've got your website hosted and your security sorted, it's time to choose an e-commerce platform. These platforms make it easy to display your products and accept payments online. You can choose between platforms such as Shopify and WooCommerce – the latter can be easily added to any WordPress site.

'Hosted' platforms, such as Shopify, don't require a hosting infrastructure, which seems like an advantage. The downside is that they limit your control over your content, along with your design and development choices.

With a self-hosted platform, you have ultimate control and flexibility over your store's content and design. WooCommerce works with WordPress and offers extensions to help you with shipping, product display options, social media marketing, data analysis, and much more. In other words, you can fully customise your store to meet your exact needs.

**E-commerce platforms make it easy to display your products and accept payments online.**

## Selecting your payment gateways

Once you have a platform and hosting in place, you still need to decide how customers will pay for your products. Choosing the right payment gateway to offer is no small task. After all, you want to be sure that your customers' payment information is in good hands.

Fortunately, popular e-commerce platforms tend to support multiple well-known and trusted payment gateways. Many of these payment options are quite affordable. For example, PayPal and PayFast are available on both WooCommerce and Shopify with no upfront costs. You'll have to pay transaction fees, of course, and there will be costs required to upgrade your subscription. For a store that's just getting started, however, these gateways can be strong choices. Some of the other trusted gateways you may want to check out include SnapScan and MyGate.

No matter what gateways you choose, it's best to opt for those that don't require a merchant account, and are supported by WooCommerce or one of its extensions. You'll also want to conduct careful research into the fee structure for each option, to avoid any surprises.

## SA e-commerce on the rise

Statista reports that South African e-commerce is expected to grow almost 9% annually over the next five years, so now is the perfect time to get into online retail. Fortunately, you now know what you'll need to start an online store.

# Four steps to grow and scale your e-commerce business

We asked e-commerce expert Warrick Kernes to share a few tips on how to grow your e-commerce business – a few secrets from someone who's been-there-done-that. Here's what he had to say.

Once your online business has been up and running for some time, you can get trapped in the monotony of the day-to-day running of the business. Here are some simple suggestions to inspire you to take action to grow and scale your store.

## 1. Increase your website traffic

When business owners tell me that they aren't happy with their sales, the first thing I ask about is their traffic. What has your traffic been like over the last three months? Where is your biggest source of traffic? Which pages are receiving the highest traffic?

As an online business owner, you need to know the answers to these questions if you want to increase your sales. It stands to reason that sales are largely driven by the amount of traffic you're getting to your site. In general, if you increase the qualified traffic, you'll increase the sales. Of course, you need to get high-quality traffic. You do this by attracting users to your site using SEO and paid ads.

Paid traffic sources include Adwords, Facebook ads, Google shopping, remarketing and display ads, and can be a great way to proactively find your customers and show them your products. This method works but it requires a budget. The downside of paid advertising is that when your budget runs out, the traffic stops. Because of this, we recommend doing a combined approach of paid ads and SEO.

What has your traffic been like over the last three months? Where is your biggest source of traffic? Which pages are receiving the highest traffic?

SEO is a long-term game: creating content that ranks on Google and draws customers to your site for months and years into the future. Good SEO has relevance and authority.

The relevance of your content determines how and when it will be shown as a search result. Well-written, relevant content will be full of keywords relating to your products and it will ideally be evergreen (content that won't date) so that the content is still relevant into the future. The authority of your content and your website determines how your site is ranked on Google.

If you can create content that is shared or linked to from popular (highly authoritative) websites in your market, this will increase the authority of your website. Building your website authority and constantly releasing relevant content is a great way to get up to the top of page one on Google. This will naturally increase your sales.

## 2. Increase your conversion rate

The conversion rate of your website shows how many visitors to your site complete an order. South Africa's average is lower than most people might think – just 1.3%. This becomes a very important metric to monitor: if your website's current conversion rate is sitting at 1% and you can increase that to 2%, you'll double your sales from the same amount of traffic.

CRO (Conversion Rate Optimisation) is a never-ending game of tweaking and fine-tuning your website to see what works best. Not sure where to start? Here are a few key areas:

- Check the logic of your website navigation to ensure that users can find the product that they're looking for in as few clicks as possible.
- Ensure the checkout process has zero distractions or pop-ups.
- Check that your 'Add to Cart' button is an eye-catching colour.
- Ensure that your site works 100% perfectly on a smartphone.
- Set up abandoned cart recovery emails (if a customer doesn't complete their purchase, you send them an email reminder to complete check-out).
- Put some budget into remarketing to bring interested users back to buy.

# 3. Increase your average order value

Every time you're in a queue at the shops, you'll see the sweets and magazines strategically placed to encourage impulse purchases and increase the value of your order. Imagine how much those R25 impulse purchases add to the company's overall annual turnover!

If you're not already doing this on your website, it's a simple addition that can lead to an overall increase in sales. There are many ways to encourage customers to increase their order value. Depending on which website platform you're on, there are several plug-ins and apps that recommend up-sell and cross-sell products. You can structure bundle deals, offer buy-X-get-Y deals or you can offer a gift with purchase if the customer upgrades to the more expensive alternative.

If you offer free shipping on orders over R500, then you prompt customers to add something to their cart when they're buying something for R450. This works exceptionally well and helps to drive up the average order for your store.

# 4. Leverage marketplaces to grow your sales

Instead of seeing the big retailers as our biggest competition, we can now start using them to our advantage. By listing and selling your product through marketplaces (like Takealot, Loot, Makro and Bid or Buy), you can get massive exposure for your products to the millions of people that visit these sites regularly. As a result, you may be able to significantly grow your sales.

Some entrepreneurs are hesitant to list their products on marketplaces because of the fees involved, and because they don't want to cannibalise sales on their own sites. But the truth is that customers who buy from big marketplaces probably wouldn't have found your site independently, so these are sales that you wouldn't have had otherwise. Of course, it is important to check that your margins allow for you to sell through the marketplaces and still make a profit at the end of the day.

These are just four ideas to grow and scale your e-commerce business. For more tips on how to increase your online sales and to learn more about e-commerce in South Africa, take a look at the Insaka e-commerce community.

# Five affordable ways to promote your online store

Promotion is the key to the success of any online store. The more effort you put into marketing your products, the more likely it is that customers will decide to buy from you. Customers can't buy what they can't see.

But for many online stores, spending huge amounts of money on marketing isn't an option. Fortunately, there are a few cost-effective ways to promote your online store. Some approaches, like SEO, require some of your time, but very little upfront investment. Here are five affordable ways to promote your online store.

## 1.  Reach out to bloggers and influencers

One of the best ways to promote a new online store is to establish relationships with bloggers and social media influencers.

There are several ways you can approach influencer marketing. Here are a few examples:

- Give out free samples of key products in exchange for promotion (a review or social media mention, tagging your account or website).
- Offer to provide unique discount codes to their followers.
- Offer a free guest blog post on a topic their audience will be interested in.

"These people are part of my journey, they actually held my hand. They are the reason I'm here today."

**See this advice come to life by scanning the QR code below.**

**Agriculture and Farming Influencer**
Ncumisa Mkabile

The way you approach influencers and bloggers needs to be natural. Ensure that your products are in alignment with their brand. Focus on influencers who care about their reputation and only endorse products they genuinely believe in. This will make their promotion of your online store more authentic.

## 2. Publish videos on YouTube

YouTube is the second most popular social media platform in the world, making it a gold mine of marketing possibilities.

Some online stores spend thousands on over-produced commercials, but you don't need to do that. Use your smartphone – it's all the equipment you need to get started.

YouTube is the second most popular social media platform in the world, making it a gold mine of marketing possibilities.

**Some helpful DIY video ideas include:**

- Product showcases, where you highlight key product features.
- Tutorials on how to use your products.
- Unboxing videos, to show potential customers what they'll get when they order from you.

The best part about online videos is that you can easily use them for cross-promotion. This means you can publish a video on YouTube, social media, and your own website, all in a matter of minutes.

## 3. Create quality content

Another great way to promote your online store is with a blog. By publishing frequent high-quality content, you can help more people find your shop through search engines.

- Blogging provides you with a platform to talk about your products' benefits, as well as why you started your online store and what your brand stands for.
- You can write content that helps answer questions for potential buyers.
- It allows you to show off your expertise through product guides, tutorials, and comparison posts that feature your and your competitors' products.

Blogging is a fantastic low-cost promotion method because it's highly scalable (and easy to start if you use WordPress). You can publish one blog post per week or once a day. The more consistent you are, the better the results will be.

## 4. Improve your SEO

SEO is a collection of techniques that you can apply to get more attention and traffic from search engines such as Google. Creating strong content is the cornerstone of good SEO, but it's not the only thing you should be doing.

**Some other key optimisation techniques include:**

- Getting backlinks from reputable websites
- Crafting attention-grabbing titles and descriptions
- Using the right keywords, so that relevant users can find your store

These days, you don't need the services of a professional to tackle SEO. If you pay attention to the basics of SEO, it can make a world of difference for your e-commerce store.

## 5. Google Ads

Online promotion does require a bit of a budget, but you don't have to spend a lot to see returns. Google Ads is a highly-targeted way to promote your online store, where you can spend as much (or as little) money as you want.

Geekwire reports that Google Ads commands 73% of the market share for search advertising, which means that if you're going to spend money on one platform, this is the one you should choose. Ideally, you'll test out multiple campaigns with small budgets until you find one that works for you. Once you've struck gold, you can focus on the ads that consistently perform well.

## Promote your online store without breaking your budget

Paid promotion is a strategy that works, but at a high cost. If you pour massive amounts of money into marketing for your online store, it's bound to get attention. However, there are plenty of ways you can grow your store's business without a huge marketing budget.

All of these techniques have the potential for a big impact on your store's growth. Once your store is bringing in consistent business, you can consider expanding your marketing budget. Having tested out these strategies, you'll also have a better idea of what works for you – and your customers.

# Paid vs. organic traffic

Traffic: the one thing every website owner wants (and the one thing every driver doesn't want). When you're trying to get traffic to your website, what's the best route to follow – paid? Organic? Or a combination of the two?

## Golden rules for paid vs. organic traffic

The truth is that paid and organic traffic go hand in hand: they support each other. Paid traffic is any visitor who comes to your website because you advertised to them: this can include Google Ads, Facebook ads, Instagram or YouTube ads... You get the idea. Organic traffic is the opposite: visitors who found you organically by searching for a product or service similar to what you offer and choosing your website from the search results.

While paid traffic is a good way to fill in the gap where your organic traffic isn't performing, it can't be your only technique to get visitors to your website. Paid traffic is immediate: as soon as your ads start running, you'll see traffic. It's also more manageable because you can target your visitors very carefully. But it's expensive – you are literally paying for every person who visits your website.

Organic traffic, on the other hand, is more of a slow-burn project. You need to carefully craft content that answers the questions your visitors are asking (that's content marketing). You need to work on your SEO, and ensure your site structure makes sense and that people can seamlessly move through your website sales funnel. While this might sound like a lot of work, these are all time investments that will reap big rewards in the future. They are absolutely worth spending time on because they improve the experience for your visitors (and potential customers).

## Does paid advertising work for everyone?

Yes, it does – with a caveat: you need to make sure you're doing it right. It can get very expensive depending on what market you're operating in, and if you don't understand what you're doing, you can spend a lot of money targeting the wrong people. But in short, paying for more eyeballs on your website is almost always a good idea.

The question, then, is where to start. Google Ads, Facebook ads, Instagram, LinkedIn? That depends on your marketing requirements, and where your audience is spending their time. There is no wrong or right place to get started. If you're selling beautiful vintage clothing, Instagram would be an obvious fit. Business coaching services would live more naturally on LinkedIn, while local pet grooming or products could be either Facebook (targeting local neighbourhood groups) or Google (targeting specific searches).

## Does paid advertising guarantee traffic to your site?

Paid advertising is not a golden bullet, unfortunately. If your ads aren't optimised or targeted correctly, or if you're underspending, then your ads won't be shown to the right people (or in the necessary volume) and you won't get as much traffic as you could.

Remember, too, that even if paid advertising improves traffic, it may not result in sales. You're not guaranteed to bring in the right audience. That's why it's so important to measure the quality of the traffic you're bringing to your website, by tracking conversion rates.

Building a thriving online business is a long process. It's not something you can magically fix by throwing some budget at paid advertising, but that doesn't mean paid traffic isn't worth investing in. With the right balance of organic and paid traffic, you'll be able to see the results of all your hard work paying off.

# To Do List: get your business listed

Reading this book offers a great time to assess. Take a step back, look at all your marketing efforts, examine your content strategy, and see if there are any gaps you could easily fill. One of those might be business listings: is your business listed on all the relevant platforms? Are you collecting reviews in all the places you could be?

Here's a quick checklist – but remember! This isn't a 'set and forget' process: if you're gathering feedback online, you need to monitor it, respond to any feedback (positive or negative) and be engaged in the process. If that seems like too much work to maintain, just choose one platform to begin with.

**Is your business listed on all the relevant platforms? Are you collecting reviews in all the places you could be?**

# Google My Business

Google My Business is a business listing on Google that lets you connect with potential customers. This free service includes Google Search and Google Maps, so if you have a physical store it's a no-brainer: your customers will be able to find you on the map, along with store opening hours, your contact details and photos of your products. But even if your business is purely online it's helpful to have a Google My Business listing: you can choose not to show your address but list the areas you serve. Anything that makes it easier for potential customers to find you online is helpful.

# Google reviews

Reviews on Google appear next to your company listing and can be a valuable way to build trust with new customers. You can ask your current customers to leave a review and a rating on Google reviews, and respond to the reviews once your business has been verified (a process that currently involves Google sending a postcard to your mailing address, which can take 22 days!)

# Facebook reviews

Facebook reviews are another excellent way to build trust with future customers. If someone compliments you on your service or product, ask them to leave you a review on Facebook. As you collect reviews and ratings, your business page will display a star rating out of five stars – an authentic way of knowing if you are meeting the standards you aim for.

# HelloPeter

One of South Africa's top review sites, HelloPeter lets people "learn from other people's experiences and make smarter choices". It's a great place for people to give authentic reviews of your service, and for you to respond. Again, because it's other people talking about your business, it holds real weight with potential customers.

# LinkedIn

And finally, make sure your business has a LinkedIn page. There are two main reasons for this: the first is so that your employees can be linked to your company (and not another one with a similar name). Every time anyone who works for your company connects with someone new, they are invited to follow the company page – it's an easy win. Having a LinkedIn page also lets customers talk about the good service they received or the excellent products you create and tag you so that others know who to contact if they're interested in something similar. And it's another platform to share the content you create, the services you offer, or the products you sell.

How many of these listing services are you using? How many do you think you should be using?

# Napkin notes:
# Growing your online business

1. E-commerce platforms enable you to quickly and easily set up shop on the web – even if you've never done it before.
2. To grow and scale your business, look at increasing website traffic, increasing your conversation rate, increasing your average order value and leveraging marketplaces to grow your sales.
3. Promotion is the key to the success of any online store. The more effort you put into marketing your products, the more likely it is that customers will decide to buy from you.
4. Building a thriving online business is a long process. It's not something you can magically fix by throwing some budget at paid advertising, but that doesn't mean paid traffic isn't worth investing in.
5. If you're gathering feedback online, you need to monitor it, respond to any feedback (positive or negative) and be engaged in the process.

## 07

# E-commerce in South Africa

# E-commerce website options in South Africa

With a population of more than 58 million, we all know that South Africa is a large consumer market with a growing e-commerce sector. We asked professional web developer Felix Norton and e-commerce expert, Warrick Kernes, for their top e-commerce tips.

"When it comes to choosing an e-commerce platform to build your site on, entrepreneurs in SA should only choose between WordPress or Shopify. These platforms are the most established, offer the widest range of support and both have a wide range of plugins and apps that allow you to add extra functionality to your website as you grow which means you won't need to hire a developer every time you want to make a change."

Warrick Kernes, CEO of Insaka eCommerce Academy

## 1. Prioritise the most popular product categories

According to the International Trade Administration, the top e-commerce product categories in South Africa are clothing/apparel and media. If your business operates in any of these areas, you're ideally placed to sell to South African customers.

> "The number one thing to think about when starting an online store is choosing the right product. Unlike physical stores, you need to take into account the logistics. Factor in the shipping weight, size, delivery distance and how perishable your product may be."
>
> Felix Norton, Managing Director of Woww

## 2. Support South Africa's preferred local payment methods

If customers can't pay using their preferred methods, they're likely to abandon their online shopping cart. In South Africa, 41% of all e-commerce transactions are completed using a credit or debit card, while Electronic Fund Transfer (EFT) accounts for another 20%.

Due to an increase in credit card fraud, the Payment Association of South Africa mandates the use of 3D Secure. This means your store must implement 3D Secure at checkout.

Many popular e-commerce platforms support EFT and card payments, including WooCommerce and Shopify. By choosing a platform that supports these gateways out of the box, you can reduce the time and effort required to launch your online store. Alternatively, you can process payments using a mobile solution like Snapscan. This popular app removes the need for cards and EFTs, which can positively impact your conversions and cart abandonment rates.

"As a WordPress web design agency owner, my go-to platform is WooCommerce. It's also the most popular e-commerce platform in the world, with 26% market share. I recommend WooCommerce as it's easy to use, cost-effective and well supported."

Felix Norton, Managing Director of Woww

## 3. Optimise for local search engines

SEO is vital for driving traffic to your online store but you may want to think about localising your store for the South African market. One of the easiest ways to do this is to make your site multilingual. By creating Afrikaans/isiZulu/isiXhosa and English versions of your store, you'll stand the best possible chance of getting your store indexed in popular South African search engines.

"Lean on the e-commerce community. You're not alone. This can be a lonely journey if you try to figure it all out on your own – there are already thousands of people on the same journey and you should lean on them to find the answers to your questions."

Warrick Kernes, CEO of Insaka eCommerce Academy

## It's time to become South Africa's next e-commerce success

Taking your business online can be a daunting prospect. But you're not alone in it. By creating an e-commerce store that's localised and optimised for the South African market, you'll be in an ideal position to connect with a huge (and expanding) audience of online shoppers!

# Choosing the right payment gateway

One of the most important decisions you'll make for your e-commerce business is the payment gateway that processes your transactions. This choice needs to be secure, trusted and an enjoyable experience for your customers. You also want it to be cost-effective.

It's important to choose a respected and well-known payment gateway as this helps build trust and credibility with your customers. While other options could be more affordable, you risk potentially losing customers if they're sceptical of your chosen method.

With nine years of experience building over 400 websites, Felix Norton has some helpful advice to share about choosing the right payment gateway.

## Why is choosing a payment gateway so important?

Your payment gateway is the software your website uses to process payments securely. These interfaces make it easy for customers to pay for your goods and services online. Different providers offer different payment options and you should take this into account when choosing your preferred provider.

Even though many processes are working in the background, you want to give your customers the impression that their transaction is quick and hassle-free.

If this process takes too long or involves too many steps, your customers may abandon your website at the most crucial stage in the journey. Some shoppers may be hesitant to share their payment information online, so it's also vital that you meet important security standards, including installing a Secure Sockets Layer (SSL) certificate.

**Consider these aspects:**

- Which payment methods your customers prefer to use.
- Transaction costs.
- How your e-commerce platform and payment gateway work together.
- Security. This is non-negotiable.
- A good customer experience. Also non-negotiable.

## An important e-commerce decision

There are a few popular South African payment gateways to choose from:

- Yoco charges a transaction fee.
- PayFast charges a flat percentage and a fixed fee per transaction.
- Peach Payments charges a flat percentage and a fixed fee per transaction.

Alternatively, you can process payments using a mobile solution like SnapScan. This popular app removes the need for cards and EFTs, which can positively impact your conversions and cart abandonment rates.

## Make sure your payment partner suits your business

When choosing a payment gateway, it's important to find a provider that works well with your business and the type of products you sell. Choosing a set-up that isn't suited to your business could end up costing you. Literally. Some transaction fees can end up costing you between 3% and 18% of your sale price. This can mean the difference between making a profit or not.

Your payment gateway – like your web hosting provider – should be a partner in your success. With the right decision-making process, they will be.

# Order fulfilment: a how-to guide

- Got a tried-and-tested product to sell? Check.
- Built a fully functional e-commerce website? Check.
- Ready for business? Not quite. To run a successful e-commerce business, you need to know how to streamline your order fulfilment process.

## What is order fulfilment?

Although it might sound like just another business buzzword, order fulfilment plays a critical role in the success of any e-commerce business. It's the process of receiving an order, packaging it and making sure it reaches your customer's hands – as simply and speedily as possible.

> "The number one thing e-commerce entrepreneurs should focus on is marketing. The rest – fulfillment, stock management, packaging – there are so many affordable professional services out there that you can and should rely on, so that you can focus on your one main thing: getting customers."

**See this advice come to life by scanning the QR code below.**

**Founder of Parcelninja.com**
Justin Drennan

The order fulfilment process may sound as straightforward as putting a product in a box and handing it over to a courier company, but there are typically five steps involved.

# Step 1: Storage and inventory

Are you storing your inventory yourself? You'll need to have adequate storage space or a warehouse where you can keep the products you're selling. You'll also be responsible for managing your stock. If you're not up for all of that, you can outsource storage and inventory to an order fulfilment partner, who will usually handle steps two to five for you as well.

# Step 2: Processing the order

A customer has just placed an order! Now it's time to process it. This involves picking out the (various) items ordered, moving the products to your packing station and doing quality control. You'll need to make sure none of the items has been damaged during the picking process.

# Step 3: Packing the order

Now it's time to pack the order. Make sure you use the correct packing materials based on what you're sending so that the products are protected during shipping. Do your research and work out what you'll need, whether it's boxes, packing tape or bubble wrap. You'll also need waybills, which your courier company will provide.

# Step 4: Shipping the order

When you get to this stage, it's time to contact a third-party courier who will deliver the order(s) for you. Work with a courier company that's reliable, adequately insured and professional.

# Step 5: Handling returns

A customer's experience when returning a product is almost more important than their experience when placing an order. Why? Because after-sales service is invaluable. You don't want to leave customers feeling like you're there for them while they're buying products but not when they're returning something. Make sure your returns process is simple – for you and your customers. Check that this policy is visible on your website, and easy to understand.

# Three types of fulfilment

The fulfilment type you choose will depend on what stage your business is at (whether you're just starting out or fully established) and what you're selling. These options include:

## 1. In-house

This is when you're responsible for all inventory storage and order fulfilment yourself. To do this, you'll need warehouse space, stock keeping software, automation and staff to help you pick, sort and pack. More often than not, this is how all small e-commerce businesses start!

## 2. Third-party

Outsourcing your order fulfilment to a third-party is normally better suited to businesses that are already turning a profit, with a stable cash flow. Outsourcing can be expensive but it can also save you time and effort if you're too busy to take on the back-end of the business, or if you don't have storage space, equipment or delivery infrastructure in place.

## 3. Dropshipping

This method is used when you don't keep the products you're selling in stock on your premises. Instead, you buy the product you're reselling directly from a third-party manufacturer, wholesaler or another retailer. In short, you act as a storefront where customers visit and order from. Once an order has been placed, you invoice the customer, and the drop shipper charges you. You never actually handle the products.

# Common order fulfilment challenges – and solutions

Customer satisfaction should always be your primary concern, especially when it comes to order fulfilment. Some common challenges – and possible solutions – include:

# Shipping delays

### The challenge:

Slow or unreliable shipping speed or delays can be problematic for you and affect your customers' service experience.

### The solution:

Spend time creating a fast, streamlined and efficient fulfilment and shipping process. Make sure your promised delivery times are realistic – especially as your business scales. Communicate with your customers and as soon as you're aware of any delays, let them know. Be sure to include tracking numbers in your correspondence so customers can track their orders if they want to.

# Disorganised returns

### The challenge:

You need to be able to handle returns, whether it's because a customer didn't receive what they were expecting, or the item was damaged. Whatever the reason, when a product is returned, you need to be able to accept, evaluate, refund (if necessary) and restock the goods quickly.

### The solution:

Customers expect a hassle-free return policy. Make sure your returns policy is visible on your website and easy to understand. Again, communicate with customers at every stage of their returns journey. To reduce any losses, streamline your return-related operations – an automated return management system can help.

# Free shipping expectations

### The challenge:

These days, consumers expect free shipping. For bigger, already established businesses, offering free shipping may not be much of an issue. But for start-ups and small-to-medium enterprises, offering free shipping could affect your budget and profit margins.

### The solution:

You can consider offering free shipping on orders over a certain value. And shop around – you might be surprised to find a small local courier company that's far more affordable than the big names.

# Damaged products

### The challenge:

Accidents happen, but managing the costs of refunding damaged products can result in a loss of revenue.

### The solution:

Spend time researching the best way to package your products correctly to prevent damaged goods. Consider using sturdier boxes or wrapping items individually in one box.

# Poor customer service

### The challenge:

If customers receive a poor customer experience from you, they likely won't buy from you again. Moreover, they may leave an unfavourable review that could deter potential future customers and harm your business's reputation.

### The solution:

You might not be able to afford to hire additional staff members to handle customer queries, but you can work at providing an easy ordering experience with a simple checkout system. Find ways to answer customer questions quickly and efficiently. If you're able to, consider using an artificial intelligence-enabled chatbot on your website, that can answer basic questions. Or revisit your FAQ section and make sure it's up to date, easy to find and clear to understand.

Order fulfilment plays a critical role in the success of your e-commerce business. It includes everything from receiving an order, packaging it and making sure it reaches your customer's hands – as simply and speedily as possible.

# Napkin notes: E-commerce in South Africa

1. Carefully consider which products you want to sell before you set up your e-commerce store.
2. You may want to consider optimising for local search engines by translating your store.
3. Your payment gateway needs to be secure, trusted and an enjoyable experience for your customers. You also want it to be cost-effective.
4. When choosing a payment gateway, it's important to find a provider that works well with your business and the type of products you sell.
5. To run a successful e-commerce business, you need to know how to streamline your order fulfilment process.

# 08

# All the red tape

# An introduction to website security

As a website owner, you know how important website security is – and the potential brand and financial repercussions if your site goes down. But website security is so much more than that – it's about keeping your online information safe: not just the information on your website, but your social media accounts as well. More often than not, your social media accounts are an important extension of your identity or brand. But they also contain lots of personal data, which makes keeping these accounts secure even more critical.

## What website security is (and why it's important)

Website security is about ensuring your online content is protected against cyber attacks. While everyone on the internet faces the chance of a variety of threats, from hacking attempts to malware infections, there are a few best practices you can implement to protect yourself. Your hosting provider will also implement server-level security measures.

As a business owner, you'll want to prioritise the safety of your audience. This is especially important if you're running an e-commerce site that stores customer data. You need to make sure you're doing everything you can to prevent your customers' sensitive information from being accessed by hackers or leaked on the web. You should also make sure you're fully compliant with the privacy laws.

"You need to make sure you're doing everything you can to prevent your customers' sensitive information from being accessed by hackers or leaked on the web."

We asked the IT security experts at ZeroFOX for a few proven online security best practices. Here are their best tips for safeguarding your site (and social media accounts) from common online threats.

## 1. Set up Two-Factor Authentication (2FA)

With 2FA enabled, a hacker would need access to your phone (or similar device) and your password to access your account. This adds an extra layer of protection.

## 2. Use strong passwords and change them regularly

You should create a strong, unique password for every platform you use. One for your website and one for each social media channel. You should also update these passwords regularly. Never use a single password across all your accounts. When you're creating passwords, use long, random words with a mix of numbers, letters, and symbols.

## 3. Protect your passwords

It's not enough to just create strong passwords and change them often. You also need to practice correct password management. In 2020, Wordfence blocked over 90 billion malicious login attempts on WordPress sites. It's never recommended that you share passwords but if you absolutely have to, only use a password management tool like LastPass.

## 4. Keep an eye out for phishing scams

Hackers are constantly coming up with clever ways to trick individuals into sharing their sensitive data like credit card details and passwords in phishing scams. If you know what to look out for, these scams are easy to spot. Phishing emails often contain typos and grammar mistakes and have an email address that doesn't match the sender name. Also, remember a trusted source will never ask you to change your passwords or provide your bank account details through a link in an email.

## 5. Choose a reliable hosting provider

A good hosting provider will offer several security measures to help protect your business against cyber attacks. When shopping around, be sure to look out for things like a Web Application Firewall (WAF) that gives your site an extra layer of protection. Also, something as simple as automated data backups can help you restore your site if anything goes wrong.

The right website security practices help protect your site against hackers and other attacks. They can also safeguard the privacy of your site's data and its users. In brief, website security can help protect your business reputation which, as we all know, is priceless.

# Important legal considerations for your online business

We asked the experts from Michalsons law firm to share the most important legal considerations for online businesses. Here's what they had to say.

You've come up with your online business idea and planned your product or service offering. Good work! Now it's time to think about the laws that may affect you.

Despite the boom in online business over the last decade, many people still aren't comfortable with buying goods or services online. The crucial reason is that consumers find it difficult to trust online businesses because of fears about privacy and security.

**Building a good online business and brand means considering all the relevant legal aspects.**

Across the globe, regulators have stepped in to create trust by enacting various laws that protect consumers and regulate online businesses. Building a good online business and brand means considering all the relevant legal aspects.

# Types of online businesses

Understanding how you relate to your customers is the crucial first step in building your online business. Before you think about contracts, it's essential to understand precisely what type of relationship you have – and what responsibilities.

A clear understanding of the relationship will help you focus on the laws, contracts, and general considerations that are relevant to your business. There are different types of online businesses, each with different responsibilities.

### 1. An online store may sell physical goods.

For instance, Plant Gardening Supplies provides delivery of seedlings to gardeners at home. They deliver the seeds either through couriers from their physical store or directly from the supplier via dropshipping.

### 2. An online service might provide consulting services.

Leaf Gardening Consulting is a business that provides bespoke gardening advice to its users over video conferencing software like Zoom.

### 3. An online platform may take the form of a marketplace.

Like Lotus Garden Planner, a marketplace that connects gardeners with landscapers.

# Legal terms

There is no all-purpose solution for legal terms, primarily because of how unique and intricate your relationships might be. That said, there are a few standard business models that can benefit from the same general kinds of legal terms. You will need to get specific guidance on how to tweak these terms for your use.

# The most common legal terms for online businesses:

- **Terms of use**

  The simple terms and conditions that cover people who visit your website, before they become your customer.

- **Terms of service**

  More complex terms that cover the legal relationship between you and your customer.

- **Orders**

  A separate document or web form that covers the specific commercial terms relating to a transaction, and that incorporates the terms of service by reference.

## Acceptable use

Acceptable use policies are recommended for any online business that has a social component. This component could be a feature of your service (for example, where users can interact with each other), or a community group on a third-party social media platform. This policy describes the way that your customers are (and are not) allowed to engage with your service. It sets clear rules of engagement, preventing unwelcome content like hate speech or discrimination. Describing and enforcing these rules is an important legal consideration.

## Privacy

Privacy is the set of obligations that businesses have to protect personal data from unwanted observation or disruption, among other things. The customer's privacy should be front and centre for online businesses and fully compliant with the privacy laws (the GDPR in the EU and POPIA in South Africa). If South African online businesses are trading internationally and processing the data of EU-resident data subjects, they will have to comply with the GDPR as well as POPIA.

# Privacy policy

Even the most simple online store collects a name, email address, and physical address to process an order. This collection includes personal data which the law requires you to protect and process lawfully. A privacy policy lets your customers know that you are protecting their personal data, and legitimises your online business.

**A privacy policy lets your customers know that you are protecting their personal data, and legitimises your online business.**

# Cookie policy

Cookies are small text files that websites put on your device to track you. They've been around for a long time, but there has recently been a high-profile law in Europe that regulates how they work in the form of the PECR or ePrivacy Regulation. These laws oblige websites to get consent to put cookies on their customers' machines. This is usually in the form of a pop-up or a notice letting visitors to your website know that cookies are being collected.

# PAIA manual (Promotion of Access to Information Act)

South Africa's access to information law defines how people can get information from your organisation. Recently, the law on who needs a PAIA manual has changed. Now, all businesses require PAIA manuals.

> "As the volume of data we collect as businesses grows, there is a responsibility to maintain the free flow of information, in a protected and secure way."

See this advice come to life by scanning the QR code below.

**Founder of Whipping The Cat**
Graeme Wilson

## Data processing agreements

Data processing agreements are relevant because your organisation is not an island. You are often processing personal data together with other organisations. Data protection law generally requires a data controller to enter into a written agreement with their processors to regulate how they process personal data on their behalf. Precisely what that agreement contains depends on the relevant data protection law. POPIA and the GDPR require that the processor follow the controller's instructions and secure the personal data they process on their behalf against unauthorised access.

## Security

Security is another critical issue for online businesses. It's essential to have the necessary safeguards in place to keep your systems and data free from danger, threat or harm.

# Returns and refunds

A returns policy is most necessary where you are an online store selling physical goods to consumers. The Consumer Protection Act (CPA) and Electronic Communications and Transactions Act (ECTA) give consumers a variety of ways to return goods. A policy acknowledging these helps to build trust with your customers and avoids unnecessary arguments.

"Security is another critical issue for online businesses. It's essential to have the necessary safeguards in place to keep your systems and data free from danger, threat or harm."

# Marketing

Direct marketing includes email newsletters or SMS messages. Previously, a business could send direct marketing messages to prospects in South Africa, provided they allowed the recipient to opt out. Since POPIA has taken effect, this has changed.

Under POPIA, section 69(3), you may communicate via electronic means (emails, instant messaging) with customers if you:

- Obtain their details in the context of a sale of products or services; and
- Market your similar goods or services.

You can only market to your customers (under this provision) if you also meet the requirements in section 69(3)(c). In essence, this section says the client must be able to object:

- When you collect their personal information; and
- On each communication that you send to them.

Only once you've complied with all the requirements above can you market to a customer. The opportunity to object means giving your customers the ability to unsubscribe.

While these guidelines might sound excessive to small e-commerce businesses in South Africa, remember that they are there to protect us as consumers. If you can put the right processes in place as a small business, you'll be able to grow and flourish with ease.

# Top tips for managing personal data

We asked John Giles, a lawyer from Michalsons law firm, to share the most important tips for small businesses that need to manage personal data and privacy. Here's what he had to say.

As a small business owner, the list of things you're responsible for can seem endless. If your business processes personal data, one of the most important items on your list should be how to protect this sensitive information. Here are the most helpful tips for small business owners as your requirements are very different.

## The impact on your business

The impact of data protection will differ from one business to another, depending on the amount of personal data your business processes. If you sell ice cream to the public from a physical store, you probably won't need to ask for (or store) any of your customers' personal data. The impact on your business in this example is low. However, if you're developing an app that helps people get fit and stay healthy, you'll require a lot more personal data. In essence, if processing personal data is a key part of your business model, the impact of data protection and privacy on your business will be high.

## Small business exemptions

There are many things that small businesses are (or should be) exempt from having to do. Don't get caught up doing things you don't have to. For example, you probably don't need a data protection officer or an active information officer, and you almost certainly don't need a record of your processing activities. Over time, the information regulator may increase the exemptions for small businesses.

In essence, if processing personal data is a key part of your business model, the impact of data protection and privacy on your business will be high.

## Focus on the important things

Focus on the essentials for your business. If you have a mailing list for email marketing that brings in lots of business, make sure you're getting it right: enable people to opt out and be careful who you add to the list. If you're a B2B business and you process personal data for other businesses, be sure to build trust by assuring them that you protect the personal data you process for them. The clauses in your contract dealing with personal data, confidentiality and intellectual property will be important.

The reason the law wants you to protect personal data is to protect people from harm.

# More than a privacy policy and training

Many organisations think that data protection compliance means having a privacy policy and training their employees. Those are two important aspects for many small businesses, but they're not the whole story. A privacy policy explains to your customers how you process their personal data, and what you'll do with their information, once they've given their consent. The employees who actually process this data need to understand your privacy policy and what they should and shouldn't be doing.

But data protection compliance is so much more than just a privacy policy and internal training. There are other things you will need to do: secure the personal data, compile consent forms, only transfer personal data to another country if there are protections in place, and tread carefully with children's personal data and special personal data (like race and religion).

# The bottom line

The reason the law wants you to protect personal data is to protect people from harm. Cybercriminals use people's personal data to steal their money, and payslips to steal the identity of employees. Direct marketers sometimes make a nuisance of themselves by marketing to people who don't want to be phoned. Some may discriminate against people by knowing their race.

By protecting people's personal data, you're protecting them from harm. None of us wants our actions (or inaction) to hurt others. With these tips, you'll be able to do the right thing when it comes to protecting personal data.

# The dos and don'ts
# of password management

Thanks to the internet, certain aspects of starting and running your business have never been easier. But along with the benefits, there are also potential risks. The more you're able to do online, the more passwords and PINs you need to remember, which can be overwhelming. Be careful not to stray into password management habits that aren't good practice.

Another thing to consider is what happens when you need to share passwords with other members of your team. Sharing passwords, even in a trusted internal team environment, can inadvertently put your business at risk.

Luckily, there are a couple of rules to follow that will protect your passwords.

Here are some password dos and don'ts to keep in mind when managing and sharing sensitive credentials.

## Dos

**Do** use a password management tool to keep your sensitive information in a safe location. There are a number of apps and services that will help you manage and share your encrypted credentials in one place. Choose the right one for your needs – for instance, team sharing. Well-known tools include Passbolt, 1Password, LastPass, and Google Smart Lock.

**Do** use Two-factor Authentication (2FA) whenever possible. This added layer of security requires a mobile phone number, or an authenticator app, to be used in conjunction with a password. Using 2FA is highly recommended for access to your password management tool.

**Do** use auto-generated complex passwords – most password management apps include a password generator and this facilitates the practice of using a different password for each new account.

**Do** revoke access to your accounts for employees who leave your organisation.

# Don'ts

**Don't** write passwords down in notebooks or on sticky notes. While this is tempting, it poses a serious security risk if criminals gain access to your premises.

**Don't** use the same password across multiple services. Doing so makes you vulnerable. Should a single service's password become exposed, all other services will also be accessible.

**Don't** share your passwords. You should never share your passwords but if you have no other choice, never send them over insecure means like email or SMS.

**Don't** use personal information in your passwords – it makes it easier for criminals to reverse-engineer. For example, commonly used password formats include birthdays, children's names, or company names. This information can easily be sourced by hackers via social media.

It's scary how much information we share online these days – especially if you're running a small business. But with the right safety measures in place, and an understanding of the do's and don'ts of password management, you can ensure your information is as secure as possible.

# Napkin notes:
# All the red tape

1.  The right website security can help protect your business reputation.
2.  Building a good online business and brand means considering all the relevant legal aspects.
3.  If your business processes personal data, one of the most important items on your To Do list should be how to protect this sensitive information.
4.  Data protection compliance is much more than just a privacy policy and internal training.
5.  Be careful not to stray into password management habits that aren't good practice

# Notes:

# Notes:

# Farewell – for now

So, this leg of the journey has come to an end.

You may be feeling exhilarated at the prospect of growing your online business. Perhaps you're feeling terrified? Or maybe you feel a mix of both. Frankly, you're going to feel every emotion available to you over the next stretch of this adventure. Get used to it. Buckle up and enjoy the ride, as they say.

I hope that through all of this, you're feeling at least a little more confident than when you started. Business, at its core, is fairly simple. It's about creating value. If you can convince enough people to understand that value, you will be successful.

At the same time, business is also really not simple.

There are going to be multiple threats and opportunities outside of your control. Your job is to be ready for all of it. You cannot control the environmental factors that hit you, but you can control the way you respond to them.

Jim Collins, the Stanford professor and bestselling author, talks about 'return on luck'. Entrepreneurs who seem lucky don't rely on luck to be successful. They work hard for years: preparing, learning, iterating, improving. When opportunity strikes, they're ready for it.

What does that entail?

The name 'Heavy Chef' comes from the saying 'never trust a skinny chef'. Entrepreneurship is about continual taste-testing the ingredients of a business. We learn by doing. Sometimes things will go wrong. Sometimes we use the wrong ingredients in a recipe.

It's all part of the journey.

The most important thing is to keep learning.

Keep threading those lessons into your business, through all the failures and successes.

I encourage you to tuck into the ongoing recipes that we're uploading every week onto our platform. Share them with your peers, colleagues and friends. Join us at Heavy Chef community meetups. Join other local entrepreneur meetups. Create your own, if there isn't one.

This journey needs good people to come along with you, to share the adventure.

With that in mind, I'm massively grateful to the good people that put together these chapters – Shannon, Bridget, Athena, Jenna, Louis and the xneelo and Heavy Chef crew. This is just the beginning of our own adventure together.

In the meantime, we'd love to know what you think, dear reader. When you have a minute or two, please email us at guides@heavychef.com and let us know your feedback on this work.

I look forward to hearing from you.

Peace.

Fred Roed
CEO, Heavy Chef

# Acknowledgements

Mark Peddle, Juan Stander, Jenna Laughton, Bridget McNulty, Shannon Innell, Switch, Mwabi Motaung, Fred Roed, Louis Janse van Rensburg, Kim Trollip, POD.

www.ingramcontent.com/pod-product-compliance
Lightning Source LLC
Chambersburg PA
CBHW070932210326
41520CB00021B/6913